The Dreaded Feast

WRITERS ON ENDURING THE HOLIDAYS

EDITED BY MICHELE CLARKE
AND TAYLOR PLIMPTON

INTRODUCTION
BY P.J. O'ROURKE

ABRAMS IMAGE | NEW YORK

Editor: David Cashion
Designer: Pamela Geismar
Production Manager: Jacqueline Poirier

Library of Congress Cataloging-in-Publication Data

The Dreaded Feast : writers on enduring the holidays / edited by Taylor
Plimpton and Michele Clarke ; introduction by P.J. O'Rourke.
    p. cm.
  ISBN 978-0-8109-8265-9
  1. Christmas stories, American. 2. Humorous stories, American. I.

PS648.C45D74 2009
394.2663—dc22

2009009393

THE ART OF BOOKS SINCE 1949

115 West 18th Street
New York, NY 10011
www.abramsbooks.com

CONTENTS

The Dreaded Feast

GIVE IT A REST, YE MERRY GENTLEMEN:
AN INTRODUCTION

BY P.J. O'ROURKE

"𝕳𝖆𝖕𝖕𝖞 XXXXing Holidays." Let us put aside the multicultural niceties and admit we're talking about Christmas. Chanukah was instituted by Judas Maccabeus in 165 B.C. (which is last week by Jewish antiquity standards) and was only recently ginned up to compete with the louder bells and stronger smells of Yuletide. Kwanzaa was invented in 1966 by Ronald Everett, aka Maulana Karenga, author, political activist, college professor, and convicted felon. (I quote Wikipedia.) West African harvest festivals may have served as Kwanzaa's inspiration, but so, one suspects, did Hallmark store cash registers. The Asians have their lunar new year around the end of January—really just an excuse to send out Christmas cards late. No doubt enterprising merchants in the Middle East are trying to figure out how to get Eid al-Fitr—the feast that ends Ramadan and involves toys for the children, too much to eat, and other 'tis-the-season attributes—to hold still under the mistletoe instead of roving around the year according to the Islamic calendar.

Each of these merry-making events is frighteningly overblown in its own right, and I don't mean to belittle any of them. But we all know that Christmas is the real culprit here, the true source of the mania, depression, and clinical hysteria of the Holiday Season. It's the no, no, Noel that puts the XXXX in Xmas.

There is something innately disturbing about the celebration of Christmas. Those of us with kids know that childbirth—be the child ever so divine—is not exactly a party. And all childbirth was natural childbirth in 0 A.D. One wonders if Mary made God stay in the manger with her while she called Him a selfish pig and insensitive s.o.b. and yelled that the next time there was any immaculate conceiving to be done the angel Gabriel could go blow his own horn.

It's a fraught moment no matter how many Wise Men you've got bringing you frankincense, myrrh, and a new washer and dryer. Frankincense, by the way, was used for embalming. Which brings us to the matter of how the whole Goodwill to Men thing would turn out. Jesus didn't live to be old enough to run for U.S. president. Nor did the birth of the Prince of Peace bring much of same. According to the gospel of Matthew, chapter 2, the Christ child was not yet sitting up and taking solid food when Herod began to hunt down the "King of the Jews." In Herod's opinion the Jews already had a king—Herod. The Holy Family needed to flee into Egypt. (A need to flee *into* Egypt was not a good sign and still isn't.) "Then Herod . . . was in a furious rage, and he sent and killed all the male children in Bethlehem and in all that region who were two years old and under."

The traditional date for this event is December 28th. Herod didn't even wait until the first of the month, the way VISA and MasterCard do, to begin the post-Christmas bloodletting. The massacre of the innocents was, alas, only the beginning of the death toll from *odium theologicum*. Jesus himself said, as recorded in Matthew, chapter 10, "I have not come to bring peace, but a sword. For I have come to set a man against his father, and a daughter against her mother, and a daughter-in-law against her mother-in-law . . . " In what tone of voice did Christ make this statement? St. Matthew, a solemn and unsmiling writer, gives us no clue. I'm guessing it was said with ironic resignation. If not, mankind needs not only salvation but Dr. Phil.

Speaking as a Christian myself, I can see why Christmas is depressing. What I can't see is why anybody would think otherwise. Not that Christmas is a particularly Christian holiday. Most societies, especially in the northern latitudes, have some sort of ceremonial occasion on or near the shortest day of the year. And those societies all seem to be suffering from undiagnosed Seasonal Affective Disorder, resulting in severe depressive behavior. The article "Feasts and Festivals" in the *Encyclopedia*

Britannica (the 11TH edition of 1910, when certainty still prevailed) notes that Mexico has its Day of the Dead in November, and China has similar gloomy rites at the winter solstice. "The ancient Peruvians," the *Encyclopedia* continues, "had the custom of periodically assembling the embalmed bodies of their dead emperors in the great square of the capital to be feasted in company with the people." By comparison, Christmas dinner with great-aunt Lillian at the nursing home is a treat.

At what would become Christmastime, the Egyptians performed a ritual concerning their own god of resurrection and renewal, Osiris. His evil brother Set cut up his body and scattered the parts. December was when Osiris's loving sister Isis, who was also Osiris's wife, found all the bits and pieces—except the penis. And you think there's a lot of drama going on with your family during the holidays.

The Romans are remembered for Saturnalian high-jinks, but, immediately thereafter on the first day of January, slaves were expected to give gifts to their masters and clients to their patrons—Christmas the wrong way around.

Yule and its log have nothing to do with the birth of Christ but date back to pagan Scandinavia. The Christmas tree has Christian origins only insofar as St. Boniface, 8th century missionary to the Germans, used a fir decorated with offerings to Christ as a replacement for sacrifices made to Odin's sacred oak. We can imagine what the Germans were sacrificing. Queen Victoria's husband, Prince Albert, a German, brought the Christmas tree with him to England. This explains why preteen boys, in the era when pipe tobacco still existed, used to while away the longueurs of Christmas vacation by phoning drug stores and asking if they had Prince Albert in a can. "Better let him out!"

We may owe the very date of Christmas to heathen misbehavior. The early church fathers could not agree when Christ was born. The Venerable Bede, England's first historian, wrote that "the ancient peoples of the Angli began the year on the twenty-fifth of December . . . the very night which is now so holy to us, they called in their tongue *modranecht*, that is, the mothers' night, by reason we suspect of the ceremonies which in that night-long vigil they performed." Bede discreetly omitted description of what was suspected.

Christians originally did not celebrate Christmas. In the year 245 the theologian Origen condemned the idea of marking Christ's birthday "as if he were a king Pharaoh." Origen castrated himself to ensure his own chastity and probably didn't have much fun at office Christmas parties.

Christmas began to be generally observed in the 4th century but did not become a holy day of obligation until 534. It's likely there was a church politics aspect to the fact that we have Christmas at all. The Manichaean heresy, introduced in the 4th century, denied the corporal or human existence of Christ. Christmas reinforced the orthodox view of Christ in the flesh, as a person—and an itty, bitty cute one at that.

We have confusing accounts of medieval Christmas festivities. The holiday seems to have been confounded with the day devoted to the aforementioned murdered children of Bethlehem. This was known as Childermas or Innocents' Day and it was an occasion to indulge young people and give them presents. A boy bishop would be elected. The youngest monk would take over as abbot of a monastery. (What parallels this has with later sexual scandals in the Catholic clergy we'll leave undiscussed.) Practical jokes were played and pranks were pulled doubtless involving medieval equivalents of phones, drug stores, and pipe tobacco in cans. On the other hand, Innocents' Day was supposed to be unlucky. No enterprise was begun then. And English children were whipped in their beds that morning to remind them of the dolefulness of the occasion. Christmas and Childermas also fall close to the Feast of the Epiphany (January 6th), the supposed date of the visit of the three Wise Men and of Christ's baptism by John and of the miracle at the wedding feast in Cana. We moderns with our sensitive attempts to make the end of the year ecumenical aren't the first people to be confused about what the hell we're celebrating. Anyway, in the middle ages, the season culminated with the Feast of Fools where minor church functionaries would perform burlesques of the mass and otherwise mock religion—the Bill Mahers of their day.

Whether things got better thereafter is a matter of opinion. Here's a brief description of a 17th century holiday get-together: "The Christmas feast brought in state into the hall heralded by the Lord of Misrule and the minstrels, and headed by the chief cook carrying the boar's head..." All they needed was my drunk Uncle Mike in a Santa suit to make a real night of it.

Charles Dickens, who is said virtually to have invented Christmas as we know it, has a yuck-making moment of Season's Greeting in *The Pickwick Papers*. The protagonist has been, without respect to his age or dignity, maneuvered beneath that mistletoe. "It was a pleasant thing to see Mr. Pickwick in the center of the group, now pulled this way, and then that, and first kissed on the chin, and then on the nose, and then on the spectacles..." Pass the Purell sanitizer.

The best Christmas I ever spent was in Somalia in 1992. I was there for ABC Radio, covering the very unsuccessful attempt by American and other Western military forces to bring good cheer to the Somalis. Eighteen or twenty of us—reporters, cameramen, video editors, and so forth—were holed up in an ex-nice walled house in Mogadishu surrounded by our local-hire armed guards. The ABC bureau in London had sent us an artificial Christmas tree packed into a TV camera tripod case. We erected it on the roof and decorated it with the little Tabasco sauce bottles from the U.S. Army Meals Ready to Eat. The head of ABC Radio news, John Lyons, who was in charge of the Somalia coverage, broke out a half dozen bottles of whisky he'd been saving. The pain killers were liberated from our medical supply chest and passed around. We spent Christmas night on the housetop, just like St. Nick and every bit as jolly. All around us muzzles flashed, mortar rounds and RPGs exploded, and tracer bullets arced across the sky. It was a beautiful sight. The weather was perfect. There were wonderful folks working for ABC in those days. Here was comfort and joy, if you were stoned enough. And I was. I remember thinking happily that it was as if everyone had gotten what I'd always asked Santa for—a gun. ☠

WHY I LOVE CHRISTMAS

BY JOHN WATERS

𝔅𝔢𝔦𝔫𝔤 a traditionalist, I'm a rabid sucker for Christmas. In July I'm already worried that there are only 146 shopping days left. "What are you getting me for Christmas?" I carp to fellow bathers who haven't even decided what to do for Labor Day. As each month follows, I grow more and more obsessed. Around October I startle complete strangers by bursting into my off-key rendition of "Joy to the World." I'm always the Little Drummer Boy for Halloween, a grouchy one at that, since the inconsiderate stores haven't even put up their Christmas decorations yet. November 1 kicks off the jubilee of consumerism, and I'm so riddled with the holiday season that the mere mention of a stocking stuffer sexually arouses me.

By December I'm deep in Xmas psychosis, and only then do I allow myself the luxury of daydreaming my favorite childhood memory: dashing through the snow, laughing all the way (ha-ha-ha) to Grandma's house to find the fully decorated tree has fallen over and pinned her underneath. My candy-colored memories have run through the projector of my mind so many times that they are almost in 3-D. That awful pause before my parents rushed to free her, my own stunned silence as I dared not ask if Granny's gifts to us had been damaged, and the wondrous, glorious sight of the snowy, semicrooked tree, with balls broken, being begrudgingly hoisted back to its proper position of adoration. "O Christmas tree! O Christmas tree!" I started shrieking at the top of my lungs in an insane fit of childhood hyperventilation before being silenced by a glare from my parents that could have stopped a train. This tableau was never mentioned again, and my family pretended it never happened. But *I* remember—boy, do I remember!

If you don't have yourself a merry little Christmas, you might as well kill yourself. Every waking second should be spent in Christmas compulsion: career, love affairs, marriages, and all the other clutter of daily life must take a backseat to this holiday of holidays. As December 25 fast approaches, the anxiety and pressure to experience "happiness" are all part of the ritual. If you can't maintain the spirit, you're either a rotten Communist or badly in need of a psychiatrist. No wonder you don't have any friends.

Of course, You-Know-Who was supposed to have been born on Christmas, but the real Holy Trinity is God the Father, the Son, and the Holy Santa Claus. You don't see fake Josephs and Marys in department stores asking kids what they want, do you? Face it, mangers are downwardly mobile. True, swiping a sheep or a wise man for your apartment from a local church is always good for a cheap thrill and invariably gets you in the paper the next day. And Madalyn Murray O'Hair (the publicity-crazed atheist saint) always gets a rise by successfully demanding in court the removal of Nativity scenes from her state capital on Christmas Eve. But we all know who the real God is, don't we? That's right, the Supreme One, Santa Claus.

But if you think about it, Santa Claus is directly responsible for heroin addiction. Innocent children are brainwashed into believing the first big lie their parents ever tell them, and when the truth finally hits, they never believe them again. All the stern warnings on the perils of drugs carry the same credibility as flying reindeer or fat men in your chimney. But I love Santa Claus anyway: all legends have feet of clay. Besides, he's a boon to the unemployed. Where else can drunks and fat people get temporary work? And if you're a child molester—eureka! the perfect job: clutching youngsters' fannies and chuckling away, all the while knowing what you'd like to give them.

Of course, to many, Santa is an erotic figure, and for these lucky revelers, the Christmas season is a smorgasbord of raw sex. Some people just go for a man in a uniform. Inventive entrepreneurs should open a leather bar called the Pole where dominant wrinkle fetishists could dress like old St. Nick and passive gerontophiliacs could get on all fours and take the whip like good reindeer. Inhaling poppers and climbing down mock chimneys or opening sticks 'n' stones from the red-felt master could complete the sex-drenched atmosphere of the first S&M Xmas bar.

You could even get fancy about it. Why hasn't Bloomingdale's or Tiffany's tried a fancy Santa? Deathly pale, this never-too-thin-or-too-rich Kris Kringle, dressed in head-to-toe unstructured, oversize Armani, could pose on a throne, bored and elegant, and every so often deign to let a rich little brat sit *near* his lap before dismissing his wishes with a condescending "Oh, darling, you don't *really* want that, do you?"

Santa has always been the ultimate movie star. Forget *White Christmas*, *It's a Wonderful Life* and all the other hackneyed trash. Go for the classics: *Silent Night, Bloody Night, Black Christmas* or the best seasonal film of all time, *Christmas Evil* ("He'll sleigh you"). This true cinematic masterpiece only played theatrically for a few seconds but it's now available on videocassette and no holiday family get-together is complete without it. It's about a man completely consumed by Christmas. His neurosis first rears its ugly head as he applies shaving cream to his face, looks in the mirror, hallucinates a white beard and begins to imagine that he *is* Santa Claus. He gets a job in a toy factory, starts snooping and spying on the neighborhood children, and then rushes home to feverishly make notes in his big red book: "Jimmy was a good boy today," or "Peggy was a bad little girl." He starts cross-dressing as Claus and lurks around people's roofs, ready to take the plunge. Finally, he actually gets stuck in a nearby chimney and awakens the family in his struggle. Mom and Dad go insane when they find a fat lunatic in their fireplace, but the kids are wild with glee. Santa has no choice but to kill these Scroogelike parents with the razor-sharp star decorating the top of their tree. As he flees a neighborhood lynch mob, the children come to his rescue and defy their distraught parents by forming

a human ring of protection around him. Finally, pushed to the limits of
Clausmania, he leaps into his van/sleigh and it takes off flying over the
moon as he psychotically and happily shrieks, "On Dancer! On Prancer!
On Donner and Vixen!" I wish I had kids. I'd make them watch it every
year and if they didn't like it they'd be punished.

Pre-holiday activities are the foreplay of Christmas. Naturally,
Christmas cards are your first duty and you *must* send one (with a personal, handwritten message) to every single person you ever met, no
matter how briefly. If this common courtesy is not reciprocated, never
speak to the person again. Keep computerized records of violators and
hold the grudge forever; don't even attend their funeral.

Of course, you must *make* your own cards by hand. "I don't have
time," you may whine, but since the whole purpose of life is Christmas,
you'd better *make* time, buster. We Christmas zealots are rather demanding when it comes to the basic requirements of holiday behavior. "But
I can't think of anything . . . " is usually the next excuse, but cut those
people off in mid-sentence. It's easy to be creative at Christmastime.
One year I had a real cute idea that was easy to design. I bought a cheap
generic card of Joseph and Mary holding the Baby Jesus and super-
imposed Charles Manson's face in the place of the homeless infant's.
Inside I kept the message "He is born." Everybody told me they loved
it and some even said they saved it. (For the record, I'm against donating your cards to nursing homes after Christmas. One would think that
after all these years on earth, senior citizens would have had a chance
to make a friend or two on their own. Don't do it!) This season, I'm
dying to produce my dream card that I've wanted for years. I'll be sitting in a Norman Rockwell–style Christmas scene, dressed in robe and
slippers, opening my gifts moments before I notice a freak fire that has
begun in the tissue paper and is licking and spreading to the tree.

Go deeply in debt over Christmas shopping. Always spend in exact
correlation to how much you like the recipient. Aunt Mary I love about

$6.50 worth; Uncle Jim—well, at least he got his teeth fixed—$8. If your Christmas comes and goes without declaring bankruptcy, I feel sorry for you—you are a person with not enough love inside.

You can never buy too many presents. If you said "Excuse me" to me on a transit bus, you're on *my* list. I wrap gifts for nonexistent people in case somebody I barely know hands me a present and I'm unprepared to return this gesture. Even though I'm the type who infuriates others by saying, "Oh, I finished my shopping months ago," as they frantically try to make last-minute decisions, I like to go into the stores at the height of Christmasmania. Everyone is in a horrid mood, and you can see the overburdened, underpaid temporary help having nervous breakdowns. I always write down their badge numbers and report them for being grumpy.

If you're a criminal, Christmas is an extra-special time for you and your family. Shoplifting is easier and cars in parking lots are loaded with presents for your children. Since everyone steals the checks you must leave for the mailman and garbagemen, I like to leave little novelty items, like letter bombs. Luckily, I live in a bad neighborhood, so I don't have to worry; the muggers live in my building and go to the rich neighborhoods to rob. If you're quick, you can even steal the muggers' loot as they unload the car. Every child in my district seems to get rollerskates for Christmas, and it's music to my ears to hear the sudden roar of an approaching gang on skates, tossing back and forth like a hot potato a purse they've just snatched.

"Santa Claus Is a Black Man" is my favorite Christmas carol, but I also like *The Chipmunks' Christmas Album*, the Barking Dogs' "Jingle Bells," and "Frosty the Snowman" by the Ronettes. If you're so filled with holiday cheer you can't stand it, try calling your friends and going caroling yourself. Especially if you're old, a drug addict, an alcoholic or obviously homosexual and have a lot of effeminate friends. Go in packs. If you are black, go to a prissy white neighborhood. Ring doorbells, and when the *Father Knows Best*–type family answers, start screeching hostilely your favorite carol. Watch their faces. There's nothing they can do. It's not illegal. Maybe they'll give you a present.

Always be prepared if someone asks you what you want for Christmas. Give brand names, the store that sells the merchandise and, if possible, exact model numbers so they can't go wrong. Be the type who's impossible to buy for so that they have to get what you want. Here was my 1985 list and I had checked it twice: the long-out-of-print paperback *The Indiana Torture Slaying*, the one-sheet for the film *I Hate Your Guts*, and a subscription to *Corrections Today*, the trade paper for prison wardens. If you owe someone money, now is the time to pay him back, mentioning at the same time a perfect gift suggestion. If you expect to be receiving a Christmas stocking as a fore-runner to a present, tell the giver right off the bat that you don't go for razor blades, deodorants, or any of the other common little sundries but anticipate stocking stuffers that are original, esoteric, and perfectly suited to you and you alone.

It helps to be a collector, so the precedent is set on what to expect as a gift. For years friends have treated me to the toy annually selected by the Consumer Affairs Committee of Americans for Democratic Action as the "worst toy" to give your child at Christmastime. "Gobbles, the Garbage-Eating Goat" started my collection. "That crazy eating goat," reads the delightful package, and in small print, "Contains: One realistic goat with head that goes up and down. Comes complete with seven pieces of pre-tend garbage." This Kenner Discovery Time toy's instructions are price-less. "Gobbles loves to eat garbage when he's hungry, and he's ALWAYS hungry. (1) Hold Gobbles's mouth open by the beard. Stuff a piece of pre-tend garbage straight into his mouth and (2) pump the tail until the gar-bage disappears." It ends with an ominous warning, "Feed Gobbles *only* the garbage that comes with the toy," and in even smaller print "If you need additional garbage, we will, as a service, send it to you direct. For 14 pieces of garbage send $1 (check or money order; sorry, no C.O.D.) to . . ."

I can't tell you the hours of fun I've had with Gobbles. Sometimes when I'm very bored, Gobbles and I get naked and play-play.

Over the years my collection has grown. There's "My Puppy Puddles" ("You can make him drink water, wet in his tray, and kiss you"). "Baby Cry and Dry," about whom the watchdog group warned: "Take her out of the box and she smells, the odor won't go away," and "Baby Cry for You." ("The tears don't just drop out, they whoosh out in a three-foot stream.") Of course, I still cover the winner of the first annual prize (before my collection began)—a guillotine for dolls. "Take that, Barbie." "Off with your head, Betsy Wetsy!"

No matter what you think of your presents, each must be answered with an immediate thank-you note. Thinking of what to write can be tricky, especially for distant relatives who send you a card with two crisp $1 bills inside. Be honest in your reply—"Dear Uncle Walt. Thank you for the $2. I bought a pack of Kools and then put the change in an especially disgusting peep show. It was fun!" or "Dear Aunt Lulu, I was thrilled to receive your kind gift of $5. I immediately bought some PCP with it. Unfortunately, I had a bad reaction, stabbed my sister, set the house on fire, and got taken to the hospital for the criminally insane. Maybe you could come visit me? Love, Your Nephew."

I always have an "office party" every year and invite my old friends, business associates, and any snappy criminals who have been recently paroled. I reinforce all my chairs, since for some reason many of my guests are very fat, and after a few splintered antiques, I've learned my lesson. I used to throw the party on Christmas Eve, but so many guests complained of hideous hangovers I had to move up the date. No more moaning and dry heaving under their parents' tree the next day as their brothers and sisters give them dirty looks for prematurely ejaculating the Christmas spirit.

I usually invite about a hundred people and the guests know I expect each to get everyone else a present. Ten thousand gifts! When they're ripped open at midnight, you can see Christmas dementia at its height.

One thing that pushes me off the deep end is partycrashers. I've solved the problem by hiring a doorman who pistol-whips anyone without an invitation, but in the old days, crashers actually got inside. How rude! At Christmas, of all times, when visions of sugarplums are dancing orgiastically through my head. One even brought her mother—how touching. "GET OUT!" I snarled after snatching out of her hand the bottle of liquor that she falsely assumed would gain her (*and* her goddamn mother) entry.

I always show a film in one room: *Wedding Trough* (about a man who falls in love with a pig and then eats it) or *Kitten with a Whip* (Ann-Margret and John Forsythe) or *What Sex Am I?* (a clinical documentary about a sex-change operation). When it's finally time for the guests to leave, I blatantly get in bed and go to sleep; they know they better get home, Santa is on his way.

Christmas Day is like an orgasm that never stops. Happiness and good cheer should be throbbing in your veins. Swilling eggnog, scarfing turkey and wildly ripping open presents with your family, one must pause to savor the feeling of inner peace. Once it's over, you can fall apart.

Now is the time for suicide if you are so inclined. All sorts of neuroses are permitted. Depression and feelings that it somehow wasn't good enough should be expected. There's nothing to do! Go to a bad movie? You can't leave the house between now and January 1 because it's unsafe; the national highways are filled with drunks unwinding and frantically trying to get away from their families. Returning gifts is not only rude but psychologically dangerous—if you're not careful you might glimpse the scum of the earth, cheap bastards who shop at after-Christmas sales to save a few bucks. What can you look forward to? January 1, the Feast of the Circumcision, perhaps the most unappetizing High Holiday in the Catholic Church? Cleaning up that dirty, dead, expensive Christmas tree that is now an instant out-of-season fire hazard? There is only one escape from post-Christmas depression—the thought that in four short weeks it's time to start all over again. What're ya gonna get me? ☠

A FRUITCAKE THEORY

BY CALVIN TRILLIN

This was the year I was going to be nice about fruitcake. "Just try to be nice," my wife said. My younger daughter—the one who is still in high school and talks funny—said the same thing. Actually, what she said was, "Cool it, Pops. Take a chill on the fruitcake issue." That's the same thing.

They were right. I knew they were right. It's not that I hadn't tried to be nice before. It's not my fault that some years ago I happened to pass along a theory about fruitcake I had heard from someone in Denver. The theory was that there is only one fruitcake, and that this fruitcake is simply sent on from year to year. It's just a theory.

But every year around this time, someone calls up and says something like, "I'm doing a story on people who make fun of the holiday symbols that so many Americans hold dear—symbols that do so much for warm family life in this great country of ours and remain so very meaningful to all decent people. You're the one who maligns fruitcake, right?"

"Well, it's just a theory," I always mutter. "Something someone in Denver said once."

Who in Denver? Well, I can't remember. I'm always hearing theories from people in Denver. People in Denver are stinky with theories. I don't know why. It may be because of the altitude, although that's just a theory.

Anyway, I can't be expected to remember the name of every single person in Denver who ever laid a theory on me. I've had people in Denver tell me that if you play a certain Rolling Stones record backward you can get detailed instructions on how to dismantle a 1977 Volkswagen Rabbit. A man I once met in a bar in Denver told me that the gases produced by the drying of all these sun-dried tomatoes were causing the earth to wobble on its axis in a way that will put every pool table in the western hemisphere nearly a bubble off level by the end of this century. Don't get me started on people in Denver and their theories.

The point is that nobody ever interviews the person who gave me the theory about fruitcake, because nobody wants to start picking through this gaggle of theory-mongers in Denver to find him. So I was the one called up this year by someone who said he was doing a piece about a number of Scrooge-like creatures who seemed to derive sadistic pleasure out of trashing some of our most treasured American holiday traditions.

"Well, come right over," I said. "It's always nice to be included."

He said he'd catch me the next afternoon, just after he finished interviewing a guy who never passes a Salvation Army Santa Claus without saying, "Hiya, lard-gut."

When he arrived, I remembered that I was going to try to take a chill on the fruitcake issue. I told him that the theory about there being only one fruitcake actually came from somebody in Denver, maybe the same guy who talked to me at length about his theory that dinosaurs became extinct because they couldn't adapt to the personal income tax.

Then, trying for a little historical perspective, I told him about a family in Michigan I once read about that brings out an antique fruit-cake every Christmas, a fruitcake that for some reason was not eaten at Christmas dinner in 1895 and has symbolized the holidays ever since. They put it on the table, not as dessert but as something between an icon and a centerpiece. "It's a very sensible way to use a fruitcake," I said. I was trying to be nice.

"You mean you think that fruitcake would be dangerous to eat?" he asked.

"Well, you wouldn't eat an antique," I said. "My Uncle Ralph used to chew on an old sideboard now and then, but we always considered it odd behavior."

"Would a fruitcake that isn't an antique be dangerous?"

"You mean a reproduction?"

"I mean a modern fruitcake."

"There's nothing dangerous about fruitcakes as long as people send them along without eating them," I said, in the nicest sort of way. "If people ever started eating them, I suppose there might be need for federal legislation."

"How about people who buy fruitcakes for themselves?" he asked.

"Well, now that you mention it," I said, "nobody in the history of the United States has ever bought a fruitcake for himself. People have bought turnips for themselves. People have bought any number of Brussels sprouts for themselves. But no one has ever bought a fruitcake for himself. That does tell you a little something about fruitcakes."

"Are you saying that everybody secretly hates fruitcake?" he asked.

"Well, it's just a theory."

HOME FOR THE HOLIDAYS:
A SURVIVOR'S FRIGHTENING ACCOUNT

BY CHRIS RADANT

𝕴𝔱 was the night before leaving for Pittsburgh, and Mom called to inform me that it was very cold there. I hid my shock well. I lived in Boston and it was the end of December and noticeably cold. I assured her I'd bring a coat. She said she had called four times before, and hung up when she heard "that answering machine" pick up. In one week, it will be 1990, except at Mom and Dad's house, where 1956 will never end. Before she could say "See you tomorrow," Dad interrupted to remind me to get to the airport half an hour before my flight. He said they would be waiting for me "with painted breath."

The next morning would begin the four hellish days spent with my family. Ninety-six hours jam-packed with television, eating and being treated like an idiot.

I took a coat. Even though I'm forty years old with a grown child of my own, I respond to these parental directives with the fevered, "Gimme a fuckin' break!" of a fifteen-year-old. I had half a mind not to take a bloody coat. Whenever I deal with my parents, in fact, it's with half a mind. What kind of ignoramus do they take me for? OK, OK: I should know better. But this problem doesn't reside in the domain of knowing. This one is in the gut, where only anti-anxiety drugs seem to help.

How I envy people who enjoy the company of their parents without the aid of pharmaceuticals. Of course, my own daughter is among these folks, who share common interests, tastes and even a sense of humor with their parents. But for me, it's a stiff regimen of meditation, hot baths, chamomile tea, Excedrin and lots of counting to ten. And judging from the horror stories I've heard about other people's families, mine are *terrific* parents. They are, indeed, exceedingly good and well-intended people. Very well suited to attend to the needs of *small children*. If I were a perfect person, I would readily deem this far more important than these silly little gatherings at which they still consider me helpless without their constant guidance.

They're poor but generous—when they won $500 in the lottery last Christmas, they donated every last cent to a family whose house burned down. It shouldn't matter to me that they eat cheese that squirts out of a can, or that they drone on and on about the obvious. These gripes I could perhaps keep to myself. And what better time than Christmas to give it another try?

I sat on the Pittsburgh-bound plane, running familial drills in my head. I'll find absolutely nothing edible at their house. Mom will have stocked the place with sweets, un-ripened fruit, canned vegetables and squirt cheese. They'll act as though I'm being haughty for insisting on fresh vegetables and desserts without tons of sugar in them. I'll cook with fresh garlic. Mom will hold up a dusty container of garlic salt from 1956 and think I'm snooty when I say, "No thanks, I don't mind chopping this." It'll be OK. I'll remind myself that if I don't act like it's a big deal, it'll just be a matter of grocery shopping and cooking for myself. I do that all the time.

They'll tell me I'm too skinny. They'll wonder if I'm anorexic or on chemotherapy. (Mom's hobby is illness and doom. There will be plenty of boil and hemorrhoid reports.) I will try to accept this as a primitive expression of the problem of mortality. After all, I share that problem.

Dad's hobby, creative worrying, would suck me into ridiculous conversations about terrorists, famine and compound fractures. I'll just reassure him, no matter what.

The bed pillows will be like foam rubber surfboards. That's OK, because I've packed my own pillow. Everything will have an artificial pine or lemon scent from some toxic product. It won't kill me in just five days. I'll roll with it. A frenzied eating will occur about every 40 minutes. Hey, everybody chooses their own poison. I'll leave them alone about the smoking and the squirt cheese.

Andy Williams will bellow Christmas songs from the 1956 hi-fi while Dad watches the news. Over all this, my parents will conduct a full-volume conversation—about nothing—from different rooms. And I will *be patient*.

They'll do things they've always done to drive me nuts and I won't go nuts. I'll translate every single thing into a gesture of love and concern. These are two things of which I'm certain. This time, I will exhibit a mastery over the situation. My hard-earned maturity will bridge the abyss. Yep, It's going to be great.

An awful panic overtook me at 22,000 feet. I should've never started down Memory Lane, for many more land mines awaited me than just the aforementioned. Once this list-making began, I couldn't stop it. And my resolve to handle this mounting litany of predictable torments began to shimmy, but good.

Dad, a retired airplane mechanic, will take another crack at offering me advice about my business, which is writing. (Mind you, he's the guy with "painted breath.") They'll want to know if I'm any closer to being married and thereby resembling the picture they'd hoped I'd grow into. Mom will use her "scrabble calculator" to beat me at Scrabble and then she'll rub it in. They'll mispronounce words. Mom will take her clothes off in front of me at least once. Horrible, grueling, unnecessary tidbits will be discussed at great length. I will have to learn about at least one amputation. Long-winded, bizarre theories about stupid things will rake my nerves. They won't understand why I dress this way. Mom will talk through her nose.

Oh, God. We're landing.

The airline lost my coat. I had put the very coat I had assured Mom I'd bring into a drawstring bag and checked it with my baggage. The drawstring bag went somewhere else for Christmas. I look like a local girl in Mom's dorky coat. I'm already over the edge. I've been on the ground 30 minutes.

The first of the bizarre thoughts came from Mom. She couldn't imagine that USAir would lose *one* of my bags, and not the other. I pointed out that they didn't keep people's luggage together by nametags and that this was entirely plausible. Only 95 hours to go, I thought.

On the way home in the car, Dad was so busy with the harmony part to the song playing on the all-50s radio station that he took a curve too fast and the bag of donuts slid across the dash. Mom registered a near-death experience and criticized his driving. He muttered something about "not using enough rudder," and pointed out a building where he had once had two teeth extracted. Then mom described a disgusting, seeping fungus their dog had in his ears. Nevermind that Bunky had been dead for years . . . the story will live forever.

"Uncle Freddy is a great guy, but he farts when he walks," Dad said. There is no way to offer repartee in the face of this verbal buckshot. I'm simply not clever enough. I must've seemed quite dull to them, staring out the window with my mouth dropped open slightly. Already defeated. Wearing Mom's coat.

My assimilation into their home life continued from there. And so did the riveting conversation. Mom actually read me a form letter from their insurance company. Dad reminded me again that *all* women on his side of the family had eventually developed Alzheimer's disease and were full-fledged legumes before signing off. Then he played "Dark Town Strutters' Ball" and "Anchors Aweigh" on the organ—melody only. And with the aid of that foot pedal, he created the sense that the Wurlitzer was actually lunging toward you and then recoiling only to come for you again and again. Like a large, throaty cobra. This menacing effect added an hallucinogenic quality to the gathering, which didn't seem to bother anybody else.

I fled to the upstairs bathroom where my suspicions were confirmed: I had gotten a nosebleed. It's a wonder that's the only thing that had ruptured.

Just as I was plotting a phony illness and an emergency escape back to Boston, a reprieve came along. NBA basketball. Channel seven. I convinced them to stop playing music and just watch the game. We snuggled right into a common interest. Mom criticized the Knicks' defense and a chorus of "OHs" and "YESes" began to remind us of our bond. Dad grumbled that "stuffing the ball was no god-damned talent. W'hell—if you're 6'11", *of course* you can slam it in—but that's not basketball!" And our traditional arguing ensued.

I employed the drills I had run on the airplane and changed the subject in a sudden burst of diplomacy. "How about some Scrabble, Mom?" Well, I hadn't seen her move that fast in a long time. "You bet," she said with victory already in her voice.

While we played, Dad loped out into the kitchen and dished up some pecan pie with whipped cream and a Coke, sat down at the Wurlitzer and played "Roll out the Barrel" while the *Tonight Show* theme song blared in the background. Then he took an applause-less bow and decided to spray the carpet with lemon scented anti-static stuff from an aerosol can. He sat down in a fog of that stuff and ate his pie. Mom kicked my ass at Scrabble.

Within this short time, I had resigned myself to somnambulating through the remaining visit, in the name of duty and gratitude...and yes, Christmas. I didn't think they would notice. We were all three dead on our feet now. The Zombie Family Reunion.

Without a reference point to the life I live when *I* have something to say about it, I sank into a withdrawn haze and began to think more and more about snacking. I reassured myself that I could resist the squirt cheese. I resorted to a tested and proven distraction: old family photos.

Among them, I found pictures of my paternal grandmother, my father and both brothers posing with their respective basketball teams. And zillions of pictures from the 50s, when my parents were still geniuses in my eyes. They were the ones with The Answers. No empty banter back then. Their vast knowledge impressed me for many years and I basked in what seemed like unconditional love. I saw myself reflected in their eyes with a golden glow over me. This was the source of the idea that I was actually special, which later led me to break rules, become opinionated and set myself apart from others—key features of a creative personality. Dad wanted me to work in a pizza parlor.

Those were happy times, before the deafening clash of ideology. Before I could be criticized for being single. When I ate whatever was squirted in front of me. And before the globe.

Grandpa gave me the whole world back in '55. He had no idea that he would forever disrupt the ignorant bliss that had kept our family a unit until then. I *loved* that globe. I felt a certain reverence for the plastic ball, thinking I'd never been that close to the whole world before, and now it was mine. I remember my father pointing with a darning needle to a spot near the middle of North America, and saying, "There's Columbus, Ohio—this is where you are right now." I can't express how thrilled I was by this. Because that meant that no matter where I looked on my globe, there was somebody there—right now, too. I tried to picture them, so I could fill my whole world up with the appropriate people in the right places, right then.

This led to a series of questions about other people in the world that marked the end of my parents' genius. Up to that point, Dad was an authority on aerodynamics and clouds. Mom knew the names of really fancy diseases and could spell anything. They could identify any animal and tap dance adequately around tougher questions. But right then, my world got bigger than theirs. And I developed a preoccupation with the fleeting consecutive "nows" that passed in distant places without my experience of them. I plotted to replace the contentment of home with my very own big world.

☠ ☠ ☠

"*Que Sera Sera.*" Dad was pouting. I could even tell from the way he was chewing that pecan pie. He went down into the basement where his all-50s radio was blaring, to work on another of his primitive wire airplane sculptures. When he didn't sing along with Doris Day to "Que Sera, Sera," I knew he was really steamed about something. It was me. I had declined their invitation to go to Christmas Eve services, which they insisted would be entirely up to me. I opted to stay home and watch the national news and try to remember who I was. So Dad pouted about me being a different daughter than what he'd envisioned. When I asked Mom why Dad was acting that way, she lied and said he was pissed at her. But I knew she was just trying to prevent a confrontation, a long-standing family tradition—often conducted with the Up with People Singers in the background.

So as soon as Mom skunked me at Scrabble, I took a boiling bath and a Valium to prepare for the following day. USAir delivered the missing bag with my coat in it just then. I looked at it with a weird jealousy before opening it, wondering where in the big world it had gone without me.

☠ ☠ ☠

Grazing began extra early the next morning. My brothers arrived with assorted girlfriends, wives and children. And there were fried eggs, pancakes, "crew-sonts," fudge cookies, and sticks of butter disguised as every manner of food. Mom made us go look at the long icicles coming off the corners of the shed. The kids bounced up and down. Dad recited in-flight emergency procedures. And on TV, the Johnny Mann Singers sang, "Y'gotta have heart," as only they can. Dad repeated his complaint about uncle Freddy repeating his stories. Mom told everyone about the oozing lesion of somebody we didn't know. The question, "Is Disneyland more fun that Busch Gardens?" was tossed out for debate. Dad went outside to look at the sky and missed Mom's brief history of nasty gashes suffered in our family.

Mom and Dad lumbered about the house, all swollen, like bloated ghosts, chewing as they walked. It was like the Macy's Parade of Parents. People cordially offered each other another appetizer. Bizarre theories about things flew. Dad speculated that the airport would be busy again soon because people don't get Friday off.

Christmas breakfast just sort of blended into lunch, which turned into a crescendo of dinner, followed by a deafening, corpulent silence.

Casualties of the meal sprawled out in various unlovely positions in front of the TV, horrified at what we had just eaten. Breaking the silence, a swarm of little kids flew in, begging to open gifts. This dramatization of gift-giving and receiving will be a robust undertaking. In my family, believe me, it is far, FAR better to give than it is to receive.

Last year, I got a size 18/20 dress from one of my brothers who's "born again," making him my youngest brother, I guess. He hadn't seen me in two years and figured I'd probably doubled in size, like most Radants do. He also tossed in a stocking stuffer inspirational tape, the cover of which reads, "No matter your age, the approval of your parents affects how you view yourself and your ability to pass that approval along to your children. Many people spend a lifetime looking for this acceptance the Bible calls *The Blessing*." All that year, I felt just a little bit suspicious about his gift. Like, what was he trying to say? I always felt blessed by our folks—does he know something I don't?

My niece and nephew gave me a perfectly nice black sweatshirt, onto which they had applied some sort of clumpy paint substance in a random design. I finally got it scraped off with a razor blade so I could wear it to the gym.

Mom and Dad, defeated from years of giving gifts I obviously hated, asked me to get my own damned presents last year. They gave me $100 and told me to go wild. And I did just that.

My youngest brother—the one who arrived in 1962, a few years after the globe—the baby brother who *knows me*, gave me a watch with a hologram of a globe on the crystal. That was a wonderful Christmas.

Mom's voice broke the silence with an offer no one could refuse: a round of Alka-Seltzers. And a thunderous fizzing ensued.

Later that night, I creamed Mom at Scrabble. After everyone left, I cleared the table, examining bowl after bowl of the food, which had cooled to a consistency of Jell-O infused with tub and tile caulking. It wobbled. I stood there for a moment, realizing that this is the stuff my parents are made of and that's why they wobbled in the same fashion. I looked up at both of them for a comparison and found them looking back at me, puzzled that I was standing there shaking bowls of food with that look on my face.

Then we went out to see a movie about airplanes that Dad wanted to see. I heard him muttering to the screen to "keep the nose up...air speed's too low . . ." On the way home, Dad worried that I might, someday, for some reason, be taken hostage. Mom squirmed in the front seat to show me where her back hurt. And finally, back home, I reviewed my Scrabble win. It was the healthy 120-point spread that made it such a definitive victory. I declared that I would never play Scrabble with her again so that my championship would stand in perpetuity. She congratulated me and told me that Mike Stevens had died mercilessly of a horrible brain tumor.

They took me to the airport the next day. I wore my own coat and my hologram globe watch from little bro. Dad was concerned about the plane I was taking back to Boston, and about the possibility of another ice age. I resisted turning a series of cartwheels at the airport. Any minute now, the big world would be mine again.

I looked into their eyes and saw myself again with that golden light all over me. They never understood my "alternative" ways and yet they've tolerated me all this time. I saw how much they missed being geniuses.

My heroes. 👾

'TIS THE SEASON FOR HALITOSIS

BY JONATHAN AMES

𝕿𝖍𝖊𝖗𝖊 are many upsetting things about the Christmas and New Year's season—increased credit card debt, unresolved decades-long family pain, the spiritual vacuum at the core of our culture—but exposure to bad breath is definitely high on the list.

I recently went to eight Christmas parties in seven days and I was assaulted with so much bad breath that I feel I've gone through four years' worth of dental school and I'm ready to hang a shingle.

I think this must be one of the first things dentists have to be trained for *and* screened for—ability to withstand halitosis. There's probably some kind of machine they put young dentists in front of which blows bad-breath fragrances into their faces until they grow immune, kind of like what they did to that fellow in *Clockwork Orange*, but in reverse. And the dentists who can't take the machine are weeded out and urged to find another field, but certainly not proctology.

In fact, the only people who have it worse than dentists are the proctologists. They're kind of spiritual brothers. The dentist is stationed at the mouth and the proctologist is keeping watch over the ass. I can see them talking to one another through the human body, like children communicating through two cans and a string. The dentist shouts into the mouth, "Hello, down there!"

I once went to a proctologist and desperately wanted to ask him how he could do what he did, but it was one of those questions that you simply can't put out there, though I imagine he would have said something bland like, "It's just another part of the human body."

But can you imagine looking at people's anuses all day long? And mostly at sick anuses? A healthy anus is not appealing—well, to some people it is—but unhealthy ones, the kinds that proctologists have to see, must be very disturbing, even to the most hardened proctologist.

Proctologists for some reason aren't the butt of too many jokes—because we feel bad for them?—but we always make fun of dentists. Yet have we ever put ourselves in *their* green smocks and crepe shoes? Just think of what *they* go through on a daily basis! Garlic breath! Onion breath! Rotting-gum breath! Dull-person breath!

I understand that dentists have a very high rate of suicide, and so I wonder what it's like to be a dentist in Sweden; you'd be doubly burdened. In fact, they probably have a shortage of dentists in that suicide-ravaged country. A mentally strong American dentist could go over there and really earn some cash.

I certainly couldn't be a dentist in America or Sweden. I was so sickened by this one fellow's pâté-breath at one of the Christmas parties I went to that I had to leave early. Later that night—around 3 A.M.—I bolted upright in my bed at the memory of it and couldn't fall back to sleep. I replayed the whole thing, like a barroom fight—a barroom fight that I had lost. The fellow had insisted on crowding me—we were in the kitchen of our mutual friend's home and he had me up against the sink, which was pressing on my sciatic nerve, further paralyzing me.

I should mention that this pâté-fiend had suffered some kind of injury to his larynx as a child and this forces him to whisper all the time, and at this party, which was very loud with the shriekings of overweight children and the gargling noises of alcoholics tipping beers down their throats, he had to get right on top of me to be heard. He was like a boxer getting another boxer against the ropes, but instead of jabs and upper-cuts he was scorching my face with such a fierce aroma of partially digested pâté and still-being-chewed-pâté that I was sorely tempted to behave in an antisocial manner and say:

"Listen, you're completely unaware of this, lost in the cloud cover of your own id, but you're giving me a second-degree burn with this pâté-breath of yours and I used to sort of like you, but I now feel such repulsion and dislike toward your person that I will snub you for the rest of eternity."

But I didn't say any such thing. I just took a beating and applied the St. Francis prayer: *Better to understand than to be understood, better to forgive than be forgiven.*

What made the moment a little postmodern, despite my use of an old prayer, was that not only was the fellow in question vaporizing me with pâté, he was speaking to me *about* pâté, making my living hell a sort of double hell, like two-dimensional chess.

"What *is* pâté?" he had asked as he shoved a loaded cracker like a cannonball into his mouth.

"Liver," I squeaked.

"Really? I don't like liver, but this stuff is great," he said, firing the cannonball.

"Yes, it's very popular," I aspirated.

"Is it chicken liver?"

"Most likely, though sometimes it's duck liver," I gasped.

Then I thought of a pretty duck floating around in some toxic pond and how the liver filters poison and that I was now breathing in pureed crushed poison that some pretty duck had once absorbed before being slaughtered.

"Excuse me," I then said to him, the vision of this duck floating through my mind, "but I have to go . . . "

That, I have to say, was probably the zenith of the bad breath I encountered during my holiday party sojourn. After that it was mostly just a lot of bad wine-breath with an occasional kind of universal sour-cheese smell emanating from certain people.

Naturally, I was worried about my own breath at all these parties and was trying to chew a lot of mints, and I was rigorously avoiding hors d'oeuvres, which often come loaded with breath-sabotaging ingredients.

But at one party, I noticed a fellow, as I spoke to him, pull his neck back, spinal notch after spinal notch, like a heron. I was going on about the Bush administration's attempt to quell any kind of protest and I was mostly citing John Ashcroft's ludicrous case against Greenpeace, but I could hardly make my point as I was secretly thinking that I was dousing the fellow with halitosis and that he was secretly judging me to be a disgusting person.

Oh, we're all so alone!

At another party a rather slobbish fellow spit food directly into my mouth! For some reason my own mouth was open—just for a second, I guess; it was a freak accident—and a particle of food shot right out of him and onto my tongue! It was so disgusting. We both pretended it hadn't happened, but I was deeply mortified and had to swallow the thing like the bitterest of pills.

A few years ago, some kind of white spittle shot out of a person's mouth and attached itself to my cheek and slid down, and we both pretended this had not happened, but having food shot into my mouth was even worse than that white-spittle exchange. When I got home I took three vitamin Cs instead of the recommended dosage of one, and I gargled excessively with Listerine.

At another party the ceilings were very high and no one spit into my mouth *and* I didn't encounter *any* bad breath. As this miracle was unfolding, I wondered if the high ceilings had something to do with it, or was bad breath random, like all other components of the universe? I mean what are the chances of having fifteen meaningless conversations at a Christmas party and not encountering one case of halitosis? But then again, this makes perfect beautiful sense—after all, miracles are what this season is all about.

THE CHRISTMAS PARTY
& HOW TO MIX A CHRISTMAS WASSAIL

BY COREY FORD

There are several methods of getting through the Christmas holidays. One is to board a ship in San Francisco and sail for the Orient, arranging to cross the International Dateline at midnight on Christmas Eve. As a result, the next day on the calendar will be December 26, and your Christmas will have been a total blank.

Another way to make your Christmas a total blank is to attend an Office Party the day before. . .

The annual Office party starts along about noon on December 24 and ends two or three months later, depending how long it takes the boss to find out who set fire to his wastebasket, threw the water cooler out of the window, and betrayed Miss O'Malley in the men's washroom. By the time the entire Accounting Department has been dismissed and the painters have finished doing over the two lower floors which were ruined when somebody turned on the sprinkler system at the festivities' height, the moment has arrived to start planning *next* year's party, which everyone vows will be even more hilarious than the last one. *Next* year all the guests will be supplied with shin guards and hockey sticks.

Usually the merrymaking begins in a modest way, with some paper cups and a bottle of Pretty Good Stuff that Mr. Freem, in Office Supplies, received from a salesman who was anxious to land the roller-towel concession for the following year. While a few associates drop by to wish Mr. Freem a merry Yule and sample his P.G.S., Mr. Freem's secretary receives her annual Christmas remembrance from Mr. Freem. She accepts this gift in stony silence, owing to the fact that her employer forgot all about getting her anything until the last minute, as usual, and hastily sent her out an hour ago with five dollars and the coy instructions to buy herself something she likes but not to look at it because it's supposed to be a surprise. (Mr. Freem's secretary has settled on a particularly virulent perfume, which she knows Mr. Freem can't stand.)

Precisely at noon a sound of sleigh bells is heard, and Mr. Twitchell, the boss, emerges from his sanctum in an ill-fitting Santa Claus suit, a white beard, and a jovial smile that fools no one. Mr. Twitchell is a great believer in cementing employee-staff relationships, and as an example of cooperation between the brass and the underlings he has not only supplied refreshments for the occasion, but has deducted 10 per cent from everyone's pay check to cover the cost so they'll all feel that this is their party too. After a few opening remarks, in which Mr. Twitchell puts everybody in the proper holiday mood by explaining that production has slumped so badly there won't be any Christmas bonus this year, he waves his arm toward the door, and a boy from the drugstore enters with a tray of pimento-cheese sandwiches. Mr. Twitchell beams and lights a cigar, inadvertently setting fire to his false beard and thus supplying the only genuine laugh of the day.

The next hour or so is devoted to shaking hands and getting acquainted. After all, the main idea of an Office Party is for the different branches of the organization to get to know each other better, because the L. C. Twitchell Company is really just one big happy family, and the sooner we all forget our restraint and get on a first-name basis with each other, the better time we'll have or Mr. Twitchell will know the reason why. The only trouble is that each branch of the organization has the private conviction that all the other branches are manned by imbeciles and crooks, and conversation between them is limited to such expressions of Yuletide cheer as "Well, you fellows in Promotion must have quite a drag, getting that new air-conditioning outfit for your floor," or "I hear a lot of heads are going to roll in Personnel the first of the year." To make matters worse, nobody is quite sure who anybody else is, and that stranger to whom you have just confided that the organization's weak link is the Front Office will presently turn out to be none other than Mr. Furbish, the first vice-president and a brother-in-law of the boss.

The only thing to do, under these circumstances, is to get good and loaded as fast as possible. After sufficient champagne has been mixed with sufficient rye, the ice is broken, and the celebrants are not only calling each other by their first names, but are adding certain endearing epithets which they have kept bottled up all year. For example, that mild, soft-spoken Mr. Murgatroyd of the Accounting Department has just backed his immediate superior into a corner and is telling him in a loud voice that he ought to know for his own good what people are saying about him, they all think he is nothing but a stuffed shirt and why doesn't he try and act like a human being for a change? (Mr. Murgatroyd will awaken in a cold sweat next morning and try to remember what he said.)

Little Miss Meeker, who isn't used to cocktails, is contributing to the general merriment by paddling barefoot in the drinking fountain. Mr. Trench of Sales, having pursued his secretary around the desks with a sprig of mistletoe, has cornered her behind the filing cabinet and is assuring her in maudlin tones that his wife doesn't understand him. (As a result of these confidences, his secretary will be transferred shortly to the Chicago branch.) Mr. Phinney, the conscientious office manager, is wandering from room to room with a harried expression, retrieving the stub of a cigarette which some merrymaker has left burning on the edge of a desk, or picking up an empty highball glass and wiping off the ring of moisture from the mahogany bookcase. Mr. Phinney greets the Office Party each year with all the enthusiasm he would display toward a return attack of sciatica.

By midafternoon the party is a shambles. Paper cups, parts of sandwiches, and an occasional girdle litter the floor. Four shirt-sleeved

individuals from the Traffic Department, perspiring freely, have orga-
nized a quartet and are rendering such nostalgic Christmas carols as
"Jack, Jack, the Sailor Chap" and "O'Reilly's Daughter." Miss Meeker
has passed out cold, with her head in a wastebasket, and the upright
members of the staff are drawing lots to see which one will get her
back to Staten Island. (Miss Meeker will be discovered in Van Cortlandt
Park two days later, wandering around in a dazed condition.) Several
fist fights have broken out in the men's room, and a first-aid station
has been set up in the reception hall for the treatment of abrasions,
minor contusions, and black-and-blue marks on stenographers' thighs.
Mr. Twitchell remains cold sober, observing the celebrants through
his pince-nez glasses and jotting down their names grimly in his little
black book. Tomorrow will be Christmas, and maybe Santa Claus will
leave a little pink slip in *your* stocking.

By the time the affair breaks up along toward midnight, at the
request of the building superintendent and a squadron of police, so
much ill will has been generated among the staff that it will take at
least twelve months for the organization to get back to normal, and
then it will be time for next year's Office Party.

The only solution I know is to stage an Office party of your own on
December 23, two days before Christmas. If you get sufficiently fried,
you may wander by mistake into the wrong Office Party the following
noon. Not only will the proceedings be about the same as the party in
your own office, but you won't get fired.

And a Merry Christmas to you, courtesy of the L. C. Twitchell
Company.

HOW TO MIX A CHRISTMAS WASSAIL

Use any large receptacle, such as the office water cooler, and fill with cracked ice. Carefully measure one jigger of gin. Stir (do not shake) and taste. Add a second jigger of gin, stir, and taste; add another jigger, stir, and taste; frown slightly, dump in the remainder of the bottle, and invite a couple of fellow workers to try it and see if they think it needs anything. After a brief consultation, add (1) a pint of rye, (2) the contents of a flask of scotch, (3) a few cans of beer, and (4) another bottle of gin that Mr. Trench has just located in the bottom drawer of his secretary's desk. Continue to stir and taste, adding other items contributed from time to time by interested onlookers such as (5) a fifth of bourbon that Mr. Alvord was planning to take home to his wife, (6) a bottle of brandy that Mr. Freem had intended to burn over the plum pudding tomorrow, (7) the juice from a jar of stuffed olives, (8) a bottle of rubbing alcohol (from the office dispensary), (9) the remains of a quart of champagne (from the private party in Mr. Twitchell's office), and (10) a dead cigar butt (tossed in by Mr. Akers, the office card). Alternately stir and taste, being careful to rotate the mixture counterclockwise to the way the room is revolving, in order to avoid spilling. (Note: If the room gets going too fast, lie prone on the floor and hold onto a corner of the filing cabinet until it comes around again.) Keep stirring until the water cooler is thoroughly dissolved.

Serve in paper cups, with a slight twist of Mr. Aker's neck.

THE MADONNA OF TURKEY SEASON

BY JAY McINERNEY

𝕴𝐭 came to seem like our own special Thanksgiving tradition—one of us inevitably behaving very badly. The role was passed around the table from year to year like some kind of ceremonial torch, or a seasonal virus: the weeping and gnashing of teeth, the breaking of glass, the hurling of accusations, the final nosedive into the mashed potatoes or the shag carpet. Sometimes it even fell to our guests—friends, girlfriends, wives—the disease apparently communicable. We were three boys who'd lost their mother—four if you counted Dad, five if you counted Brian's best friend, Foster Creel, who'd lost his own mother about the same time we did and always spent Thanksgiving with us—and for many years there had been no one to tell us not to pour that pivotal seventh drink, not to chew with our mouths open, not to say *fuck* at the dinner table.

We kept bringing other women to the table to try to fill the hole, but they were never able to impose peace for long. Sometimes they were catalysts, and occasionally they even initiated the hostilities—perhaps their way of trying to fit in. My father never brought another woman to the table, though many tried to invite themselves, and our young girlfriends remarked on how handsome he was and what a waste it was. "I had my great love, and how could I settle for anything less?" he'd say as he poured himself another Smirnoff and the neighbor widows and divorcées dashed themselves against the windowpanes like birds.

Sometimes, although not always, the mayhem boiled up again at Christmas, in the sacramental presence of yet another turkey carcass, with a new brother or guest in the role of incendiary device, though memories of the most recent Thanksgiving were often enough to spare us the spectacle for another eleven months. I suppose we all had a lot to be thankful for, socioeconomically speaking, but for some reason we chose to dwell instead on our grievances. *How come you went to Finlay's high school play and not mine? How could you have fucked Karen Watley when you knew I was in love with her?*

We would arrive Tuesday night from prep school or college, or on Wednesday night from New York, where we were working at a bank while writing a play, or from Vermont, where we were building a log cabin with our roommate from Middlebury before heading up to Stowe at first snow for a season of ski bumming. Dad would take the latter part of the week off, until he retired, which was when things really became dangerous. The riotous foliage that briefly enflamed the chaste New England hills was long gone, leaving the monochromatic landscape of winter: the gray stone walls of the early settlers, the silver trunks of the maples, the white columns of birch.

Manly hugs were exchanged at the kitchen door. Cocktails were offered and accepted. Girlfriends and roommates were introduced. The year of the big snow, footwear was scraped on the blade of the cast-iron boot cleaner outside the door. Dad was particularly pleased with this implement, and always pointed it out to guests, not because he was particularly fastidious about mud and snow, but because it seemed to signify all the supposed charm and tradition of old New England (as opposed to, say, its intolerance of immigrants and its burning of young girls at the stake), although he'd bought this particular boot scraper once upon a time at the local True Value hardware store. But somehow Dad had convinced himself that it had been planted here by the early settlers of the Massachusetts Bay Colony, in between skirmishes with the Iroquois and the Mohicans. He liked to think of himself as an old Yankee, despite the fact that when his grandfathers arrived in Boston, the windows were full of NO IRISH NEED APPLY signs and they weren't likely to be invited to scrape their boots at anybody's front door. A century and a half later, though, we lived in a big white house with green shutters, which Dad inevitably described as "Colonial," though it was built in the 1920s to resemble something a hundred years older.

Most of the girls we brought—a cavalcade of blondes—were judged by their resemblance to our mother, except when it seemed, as was the case a couple of times with Brian, they'd been deliberately chosen for their controversial darkness. Each of us could see how his brother's girlfriend was a pale imitation of Mom and our own were one-offs who shared some of her best qualities. The girls, for their part, must have been a little daunted at first to discover the patterns of traits they'd cherished as unique. As different as we were, we were all recognizably alike, with the same unruly hair, the same heavy-browed, smiley eyes and all our invisible resemblances, born and bred. Brian, the eldest, kept things lively by bringing a different girl every year; we called him "the Kennedy of the family." The rest of us took after Dad, who liked to say that Mom was his only true love. Mike had been with Jennifer since his freshman year at Colby, and Aidan met his future wife, Alana, before he was twenty. Actually, Brian showed up two years in a row with Janis, whom he eventually married, much to our and then his own chagrin. The second time, she threw the entire uncarved turkey at Brian's head, a scene that eventually showed up in his second play. Another year, he and Foster nearly came to blows at the table when it came out that they'd lately been sleeping with the same girl. It took two of us to restrain Brian.

Brian's personal life, with all its chaos, Sturm und Drang, was the workshop version of his professional life, a laboratory for drama. And of course he wrote about us. Mike said at the time that the phrase "thinly disguised" was too chubby by half to describe Brian's relation to his source material. His first play revolved around the death of a mother from cancer. There seemed to be a number of those that particular season, but his was the most successful. We all went down to the opening night at the New York Theatre Workshop. The play was directed

by Foster, who'd been his best friend ever since Choate, and had gone
with him to Yale Drama. We sat there, stunned in the aftermath, as the
applause thundered around us. It was hard to know how to react. In the
play, Brian seemed to be making a special claim for himself with regard
to our mother, in that the character who was obviously him had been
more loved and more devastated than the others.

Then there was the question of his portrayal of the rest of us. On
the one hand, as brothers we wanted to say, *Hey, that's not me,* and
on the other, *But wait a minute; that is me.* He'd put us in an unten-
able position. Brian was a great sophist, and if you complained about
the parallels between his life and art, he would start declaiming about
the autobiographical basis of *Long Day's Journey into Night* or point out
that "your" character had gone to Deerfield, when you'd actually gone
to Hotchkiss. And if you complained about inaccuracies—denied that
you'd ever, for example, had carnal relations with the family dog—he
would cite poetic license or remind you that you'd been banging on a
moment before about resemblances and that this clearly demonstrated
the fictionality of his masterpiece.

At first, it was hard to tell how Dad felt about it. He put on a brave
face and went over to Phoebe's, the bar down the block, to celebrate with
Brian and the cast. He seemed to be in shock. But later, in the cab back
to the hotel, and in the bar there, he kept asking us, over and over again,
some variant of the question "Was I such a bad father?" In truth, he
didn't come off all that badly, but we all had a hard time not viewing the
play as a flawed family memoir. He also cornered Foster, our unofficial
fourth brother, whom for years Dad had consulted as a kind of emo-
tional translator in his efforts to understand Brian.

"Every artist interprets the world through the prism of his own
narcissism," Foster told him that night. "He doesn't think you're a
bad father. He forgot about you the day he started writing the play. All
the characters in the play, even the ones who look and sound like you,

are Brian, or else they're foils for Brian." I don't think my father knew whether to be reassured or worried by this. Of course, he'd long known Brian was massively self-absorbed, prone to exaggeration and outright mendacity. But he seemed pleased with the judgment, repeated to us all many times later, that Brian was an artist. At last, he seemed to feel, there was an explanation for his temperament, and his deviations from what my father considered proper behavior: the drugs, the senseless prevarications, the childhood interest in poetry. For Dad, Foster's assessment counted as much as subsequent accolades in the *Times* and elsewhere.

That year, Brian brought Cassie Haynes, the actress, who played his former girlfriend Rita Cosovich in the play, although of course he denied that the character was based on Rita, and we all wondered if Rita would, on balance, be more offended by the substance of her portrait or flattered by its appearance, Cassie being a babe of the first order. She caused a bit of a sensation around the neighborhood that Thanksgiving, husbands coming from three streets down to ask after the leaf blower they thought they might possibly have lent to Dad earlier in the fall. When we heard she was coming, we all thought, Great, just what we need, a prima donna actress, though we couldn't help liking her, and hoping she would come back during bathing suit season.

Brian's play gave us something to fight about at the Thanksgiving board for years to come, beginning that first November after the opening, when the wounds were still fresh. Mike, the middle brother, was the first to take up the cause after the cocktail hour had been prolonged due to some miscalculation about the turkey. Mike's fiancée, Jennifer, had volunteered to cook the bird that year, and while she would later become our chief and favorite cook, this was her first attempt at a turkey, and rather than relying on Mom's old copy of *The Fannie Farmer Cookbook*, she'd insisted on adapting a chicken recipe from Julia Child's *Mastering*

the Art of French Cooking. When Dad attempted to carve the turkey the
first time, the legs were still pink and raw and the bird was slammed
back in the oven, giving us all another jolly hour and a half to deplete the
bar. We might have given Jennifer less grief if she hadn't initially tried
to defend herself, insisting that the French preferred their birds rare and
implying that a thoroughly cooked bird was unsophisticated. When we
finally sat down to eat, Brian said grace without letting her off the hook:
"Notre père, qui aime la volaille crue, que ton nom soit sanctifié—"

Mike interrupted him, asking how he'd like a well-done drumstick
up the ass. Dad demanded a truce, and for several minutes peace prevailed, until Dad started to talk about Mom in that maudlin way of his,
a recitation that always relied heavily on the concept of her sainthood.
Usually we all collaborated in changing the subject and leading him out
of this quagmire of grieving nostalgia, but now Mike wanted to open the
subject for debate.

"She didn't deserve to suffer," Dad was saying.

"Apparently, the person who suffered the most was Brian," Mike
said. "At least that's the impression I got from the play. I mean, sure,
Mom was dying of cancer and all, but I never realized it hurt Brian so
much to administer her shots the one night that he actually managed to
sit up with her. Maybe I'm a philistine, but it seemed to me like the point
was the one who really suffered wasn't Mom, it was Brian."

"Okay, okay," Brian said. "I'm sorry I said grace in French."

"That's not really the point," Mike said.

"Oh, but I think it is."

"I don't blame you for trying to change the subject, you self-centered
prick. But you know what? We all grew up in the same house. And we
all saw the play."

"Now, boys," Dad said.

"You, of all people, know what I'm talking about," Mike said, pointing
a fork at our father. "Let's be honest. You were freaked-out by the play."

Dad didn't want to go down this road. "I had a few … concerns."

"Don't pussy out, Dad. We've talked about this, for Christ's sake. Why are we all so worried about Brian's feelings? It's not like he lost any sleep worrying about ours."

"Actually," Cassie said, "I happen to know he was very worried about your feelings. I think Foster will agree with me."

"It's not like he shows it," Mike said.

"I think it's wonderful how women attribute lofty ideals and fine feelings to us," Foster said. "But, I'm sorry, if Brian had spent much time worrying about your feelings, it wouldn't have been much of a fucking play."

This quip might have defused the situation, but Mike, like a giant freighter loaded with grievances, was unable to change course. Brian parried his continuing assault with glib little irrelevancies until Mike eventually stormed out of the room, spilling red wine all over the Irish linen tablecloth, but the rest of us considered ourselves fortunate that it wasn't blood. Mike had the fiercest temper in the family, and he was three inches taller and thirty pounds heavier than his elder brother.

The whole exchange was pretty representative. While Brian had always charmed and finessed and fibbed his way through life, Mike had a fierce stubborn honesty and a big hardwood chip on his shoulder, which was in some measure a reflection of his belief that Brian had already claimed the upper bunk bed of life before he came along and had a chance to choose for himself. If Brian were assailing a castle, he would try to sneak in the back door by seducing the scullery maid; Mike would butt his head against the portcullis until it or he gave way. Mike's youthful transgressions weren't necessarily more numerous or egregious, but, unlike Brian, he was inevitably caught and held accountable, in part because he considered it dishonest to hide them. Brian never let the facts compromise his objective, and he seemed almost allergic to them. When he got caught with marijuana he had an elaborate if hackneyed story about how he was holding it for a friend. But when Mike decided to grow it, he did so out in the open, planting rows between the corn and tomatoes in the vegetable garden, until someone finally told our mother, who'd been giving tours of the garden, the true identity of the mystery herb. Back then, none of us could have predicted that Mike would eventually be the one to follow our father to business school and General Electric, that he'd be diplomatic enough to negotiate the hazards of corporate culture. His reformation owed a lot to Jennifer, starting that first year at Colby. It took us a long time to learn to love her—my father was furious over her sophomore art-class critique of our parish church—but there was no denying her anodyne effect on Mike.

@@@ @@@ @@@

The year before Mike nearly throttled Brian, it was Aidan's turn. He was the baby of the family, which seemed to be his complaint—that we treated him as such. That we didn't give him enough respect. The specific catalyst, this Thanksgiving, was obscure. That he was drunk in the manner unique to inexperienced drinkers—he was a senior at Hotchkiss at the time—didn't especially help his case, and sensing this, he became even more frustrated and strident.

"Just because I'm younger . . . it doesn't give *you* guys the right to treat me like I'm a *kid*. Mom wouldn't have let you. If she was here, she'd tell you."

"If she *were* here," Brian said.

"That's *exactly* what I mean. Treating me like a friggin' baby."

We all found it cute that even in his cups, Aidan had used the euphemism rather than the Anglo-Saxonism itself. He wasn't yet ready to cuss in front of Dad. Brian and Mike started sniggering, which further infuriated Aidan, who pounded his fist down on his plate, breaking it in half and cutting his hand on his steak knife, which had been freshly sharpened by Dad that morning. We all agreed that Jennifer was the only one sober enough to drive to the emergency room.

The touch-football games preceding dinner were sometimes an outlet for aggression that might otherwise have overflowed at the table, but it occasionally spilled over, as when Brian accused Mike of unnecessary roughness on the field that afternoon. At Christmas, the sport was hockey, assuming that the pond was sufficiently frozen. Our mother, who believed that exercise and fresh air were essential ingredients of the good life, had inaugurated both of these activities.

We really should have just canceled Thanksgiving the year the movie came out. Anyone could have predicted disaster. Brian spent more than three years working on the screenplay, on his own at first and eventually in collaboration with the director. (His second play, about preppy young bohemians in TriBeCa, had opened to mixed reviews and closed after an eight-week run.) Somewhere in the screenwriting process, the story had acquired a new complication, when the dying mother confides in her sensitive son about her affair with his father's best friend.

In fact, Dad's best friend lived in San Francisco, as Brian was quick to point out later, but still, it made us wonder. Mom had been popular with most of the men in our parents' circle of friends, and one husband, Tom Fleishman, had always seemed almost comically smitten. Now we started to question if it was really a joke, the way Fleishman had always mooned around Mom, or whether Brian had really been the recipient of some deathbed confession. Everyone in town had the same question, including Katy Fleishman, who called Dad in a fury after seeing the movie in September, demanding to know what he knew, and it soon became the talk of the country club. The play had been a distant rumor, but the movie was right there next door to the Pathmark store, in the Regal Cinema multiplex, which had replaced the old downtown theaters where we'd watched *Jaws* and *Summer of '42*. And it was more successful than some might have hoped, buoyed by the performance of Maureen Firth as the wife and mother. The movie played at the Regal for seven weeks. Everyone we knew went to see it.

Brian had warned us, to some extent. On the one hand, he assured us, his vision hadn't been compromised. On the other hand, accommodations had been made, nuances flattened, whispers amplified, subtexts excavated with a backhoe and laid bare. In the play there was a rumor of infatuation.

None of us, Foster excepted, had been invited to the premiere in L.A., or rather, we'd all received a phone call from Brian, who had mentioned in passing "a big industry ratfuck" and said, "I'm not even sure I'm going myself."

And none of us knew quite what to say after we'd seen it. Brian wrote Dad a letter, assuring him that the alleged affair was strictly a Hollywood plot device and had nothing to do with reality. Dad called Foster in New York and was repeatedly reassured. Mike called Brian, threatening to kick his ass, and while the conversation was hardly conclusive, Brian swore that the affair was just a sensationalistic fiction, and it seemed as if maybe we had all had our say by the time Thanksgiving had come around. We were hoping against hope that the issue would just go away; in an unprecedented move, we even decided to water down the vodka just to keep Dad from getting too maudlin.

And for the first time since any of us could remember, it looked as if we might pass a relatively peaceful Thanksgiving, having made it all the way to the pumpkin pie without major fireworks. But despite the watered vodka, we could see Dad's eyes glazing over with melancholy reminiscence.

"I must have let her down somehow," he said during a lull in the discussion of the Patriots' season.

All of us were smart enough to pretend we hadn't heard this remark, but Aidan's fiancée was still new to the family.

"Let whom down, Mr. C.?"

"Carolyn, I must've let her down. She must have needed something I couldn't give her."

"But why would you think that?" Jennifer asked.

"Oh, for Christ's sake," Mike said, throwing his napkin down on the table. "Look at what you've done, Brian. Now he actually believes it."

"Dad," Brian said, "I told you: It never happened. It's fiction."

"It's slander," Mike said. "I still can't understand why the hell you'd drag our mother's name into the gutter like that."

"It's not our mother. It's not her name. It's a character in a movie."

"A character based on our mother."

"I just must have failed her," Dad said, oblivious to the conversation around him.

"Dad, listen to me. It never happened. I'm sorry. It's my fault. I shouldn't have written what I wrote. It was the director's idea, a cheap plot device. It isn't true."

"I always thought it was harmless," Dad said. "They used to talk at parties, and I knew they had things in common. Your mother had so many interests, art and theater, and I couldn't really talk to her about those things. I knew she and Tom talked. But I thought that's all it was."

"That *is* all it was," Brian said. "At least as far as I know."

"I know she told you things," he said to Brian. "Things she couldn't tell me."

"Not that, Dad. She never told me anything like that."

"After my operation," he said, "I was afraid. I was afraid of physical, you know, exertion."

"Dad, that's enough."

"Are you happy with yourself?" Mike asked as the tears rolled down our father's cheeks.

"Well, who's for a smoke outside?" Foster said, rising from the table. Although Dad was a lifelong smoker, our mother had, toward the end of her life, insisted that all smoking be done outdoors, a rule that Dad himself continued to observe and enforce after she was gone.

A half hour after we put Dad to bed, Mike tackled Brian and got him in a headlock, choking him and rubbing his face in the snow. "Tell the truth, goddamn it. What did she tell you? Is it true?"

"I told you: It's not true. She never told me anything."

But nothing could ever quite dispel the doubt for us. Dad might have been forgiven for lying low, but he was determined to show himself on the local holiday party circuit. A week before Christmas, after three cocktail parties, he crashed his Mustang into an elm tree half a mile from the house.

Mike, who was working in Schenectady, was the first to arrive at the hospital. Dad was in intensive care. Aidan drove over from Amherst, arriving shortly before midnight. Brian and Foster arrived from New York just as the sun was rising and Dad was declared stable. We all spent the day at the hospital and that night traded shifts in the waiting room. Dad looked gruesome when we finally got to see him, his face bruised and puffy and green where it wasn't bandaged, his leg in traction. He was pretty doped up. "Don't tell your mother," he said when he saw us. "I don't want her to worry."

The doctor, who'd tended our mother in her final days, said, "It's the Demerol."

"We could all use some of that," Foster said.

💀 💀 💀

We moved between the hospital and the house for the next ten days, keeping ourselves busy with Christmas preparations. We found a perfectly shaped blue spruce tree in the woods at the edge of the lake and we retrieved the ornaments from the attic in the old boxes from England's department store, closed years before, with Mom's block letters fading on the cardboard: CHRISTMAS LIGHTS, CHRISTMAS ANGELS, CHRISTMAS BULBS. We avoided talking about what had happened or why, concentrating instead on the practical details.

The lake had frozen early that year. After lunch on Christmas Eve, we gathered up our gear, called Ricky and Ted Quinlan next door, and trudged down for the annual hockey game. It was Foster, Ted and Aidan against Brian, Ricky and Mike. Brian's team scored two quick goals.

Aidan, who had the fiercest competitive streak of any of us, started to get physical. First he hooked Brian's skate and tripped him; then he body-checked him into the rocks of the causeway. Brian returned the favor the next time he came down the ice with the puck, knocking Aidan off into the bulrushes. He came out swinging, and caught Brian in the helmet with his stick. Then he threw him down and knelt on top of him, ripping off his helmet and punching his face. By the time we pulled him off, there was blood everywhere and one of Brian's teeth was protruding through his lip.

"You bastard," Aidan sobbed. "You selfish bastard."

Brian turned away and limped up the hill, leaving a trail of blood on the ice.

When we got back up to the house, Brian was gone.

💀 💀 💀

Dad came home on New Year's Day. Aidan took winter term off from school to be with him, and Mike came over from Schenectady on the weekends. Brian called from New York to check in. Neither the fight on the ice nor his sudden departure was ever discussed again. From time to time, in his cups, Dad would ask Brian about our mother, and he would always insist that both the affair and the confession were completely fictional. Dad once confronted Tom Fleishman at the country club and he, too, denied it. But Dad could never put the question out of his mind, any more than he could walk without a cane.

Mike and Jennifer had three boys, and he became the youngest vice president ever at GE. Aidan spent a year with the U.S. ski team before marrying Alana and going back to Hotchkiss to teach. Foster, one of the most respected directors in New York, recently married Cassie Haynes, the actress who first appeared at our house as Brian's date. We go down to see his plays from time to time.

Brian moved to Los Angeles a few weeks after Aidan busted his lip. He wrote a TV pilot, and while that project died, it led to a job as a staff writer for a long-running comedy show. We can't help feeling relieved that he's not writing about the family, and Dad watches the show every week. Brian is very well paid for his efforts and has been dating a series of extremely pretty actresses. But it also feels somehow like a cheat, a big fucking letdown. After all these years of having to put up with the idea of Brian as a great genius, of knowing that our mother believed in his special destiny, we feel like the least he could do would be to justify her favor and her hopes, instead of spending his days writing mother-in-law jokes. Nothing short of greatness could justify the doubt he cast on her memory. Foster believes that he's doing penance and that he'll go back to his real work someday.

In the meantime, we haven't all been together at Thanksgiving since Dad's accident. Now, when the leaves turn red and yellow and the grass turns white with morning frost, we feel the loss all over again. It's like we were a goddess cult that gathered once a year and now our faith has wavered. It's not that we couldn't forgive her anything. But our simple certainties have been shaken. Although we will always be Catholics, we long ago gave up on the Father, the Son and the Holy Ghost. We were a coven of Mariolatry, devoted to the Virgin. Brian believed in art, but lately he seems to have lost the faith. We find it hard to believe in anything we can't see or explain according to the immutable laws imbued in science class.

We always believed in you, Mother, more than anything, but we never for a moment thought you were human. 💀

TWO THANKSGIVING POEMS

BY BILLY COLLINS

1. Thanksgiving Morning

The crossed multiple blades of the blender
set out to dry on a counter.
The corkscrew unsheathed and ready
to enter whatever cannot resist its twisting.
The carving knife waiting alongside
the sharpener for its abrasive touch,

The blue box of matches, the white candles.
The branch of dry leaves brought in
Along with vines clustered with red and yellow berries,

All of which points to the anonymous turkey,
soon to be trussed with string
but now soaking on the cold porch
in a bucket of salted ice water,
in brine, as they like to say this time of year.

And we must not overlook the oven,
radiating in a corner of the kitchen
set at first at 500 degrees
then lowered almost mercifully to 350,

still hot enough to lift the bird
into the condition of sacrificial edibility,
yet short of what would incinerate a book,
the oven that swallowed the witch and Sylvia Plath
and now the oven of our pleasure,
our forks and glasses blindly raised.

2. The Gathering, a Thanksgiving Poem

𝕺𝖚𝖙𝖘𝖎𝖉𝖊, the scene was right for the season,
heavy gray clouds and just enough wind
to blow down the last of the yellow leaves.

But the house was different that day,
so distant from the other houses,
like a planet inhabited by only a dozen people

with the same last name and the same nose
rotating slowly on its invisible axis.
Too bad you couldn't be there

but you were flying through space on your own asteroid
with your arm around an uncle.
You would have unwrapped your scarf

and thrown your coat on top of the pile
then lifted a glass of wine
as a tiny man ran across a screen with a ball.

You would have heard me
saying grace with my elbows on the tablecloth
as one of the twins threw a dinner roll across the room at the other. 💀

SUSIE'S LETTER FROM SANTA

BY MARK TWAIN

Palace of St. Nicholas
In the Moon
Christmas Morning

MY DEAR SUSIE CLEMENS:

I have received and read all the letters which you and your little sister have written me by the hand of your mother and your nurses; I have also read those which you little people have written me with your own hands—for although you did not use any characters that are in grown people's alphabet, you used the characters that all children in all lands on earth and in the twinkling stars use; and as all my subjects in the moon are children and use no characters but that, you will easily understand that I can read your and your baby sister's jagged and fantastic marks without trouble at all. But I had trouble with those letters which you dictated through your mother and the nurses, for I am a foreigner and cannot read English writing well. You will find that I made no mistakes about the things which you and the baby ordered in your *own* letters—I went down your chimney at midnight when you were asleep and delivered them all myself—and kissed both of you, too, because you are good children, well-trained, nice-mannered, and about the most obedient little people I ever saw. But in the letter which you dictated there are some words that I could not make out for certain, and one or two small orders which I could not fill because we ran out of stock. Our last lot of Kitchen-furniture for dolls has just gone to a poor little child in the North Star away up in the cold country about the Big Dipper. Your mama can show you that star and you will say: "Little Snow Flake" (for that is the child's name) "I'm glad you got that furniture, for you need it more than I." That is, you must *write* that, with your own hand, and Snow Flake will write you an answer. If you only spoke it she wouldn't hear you. Make your letter light and thin, for the distance is great and the postage heavy.

There was a word or two in your mama's letter which I couldn't be certain of. I took it to be "a trunk full of doll's clothes." Is that it? I will call at your kitchen door just about nine o'clock this morning to inquire. But I must not see anybody and I must not speak to anybody but you. When the kitchen doorbell rings George must be blindfolded and sent to open the door. Then he must go back to the dining-room or the china closet and take the cook with him. You must tell George that he must walk on tiptoe and not speak—otherwise he will die someday. Then you must go up to the nursery and stand on a chair or the nurse's bed and put your ear to the speaking tube that leads down to the kitchen and when I whistle through it you must speak in the tube and say, "Welcome, Santa Claus!" Then I will ask whether it was a trunk you ordered or not. If you say it was, I shall ask you what *color* you want the trunk to be. Your mama will help you to name a nice color and then you must tell me every single thing in detail which you may want the trunk to contain. Then when I say "Good-bye and a Merry Christmas to my little Susie Clemens," you must say "Good-bye, good old Santa Claus, I thank you very much and please tell Snow Flake I will look at her star tonight and she must look down here—I will be right in the West bay-window; and every fine night I will look at her star and say, 'I know somebody up there and *like* her, too.'" Then you must go down into the library and make George close all the doors that open into the main hall, and everybody must keep still for a little while. I will go to the moon and get those things and in a few minutes I will come down the chimney that belongs to the fireplace that is in the hall—if it is a trunk you want—because I couldn't get such a thing as a trunk down the nursery chimney, you know.

People may talk if they want, until they hear my footsteps in the hall. Then you tell them to keep quiet a little while till I go back up the chimney. Maybe you will not hear my footsteps at all—so you may go now and then and peep through the dining-room doors, and by and by you will see that thing which you want, right under the piano in the drawing room—for I shall put it there. If I should leave any snow in the hall, you must tell George to sweep it into the fireplace, for I haven't time to do such things. George must not use a broom, but a rag—else he will die someday. You must watch George and not let him run into danger. If my boot should leave a stain on the marble, George must not holystone it away. Leave it there always in memory of my visit; and whenever you look at it or show it to anybody you must let it remind you to be a good little girl. Whenever you are naughty and somebody points to that mark which your good old Santa Claus's boot made on the marble, what will you say, little Sweetheart?

Good-bye for a few minutes, till I come down to the world and ring the kitchen door-bell.

Your loving
SANTA CLAUS
Whom people sometimes call the Man in the Moon ☺

A CHRISTMAS SPECTACLE

BY ROBERT C. BENCHLEY

For *Use in Christmas Eve Entertainments in the Vestry*

At the opening of the entertainment the Superintendent will step into the footlights, recover his balance apologetically, and say:

"Boys and girls of the Intermediate Department, parents and friends: I suppose you all know why we are here tonight. (At this point the audience will titter apprehensively.) Mrs. Drury and her class of little girls have been working very hard to make this entertainment a success, and I am sure that everyone here to-night is going to have what I over-heard one of my boys the other day calling 'some good time.' (Indulgent laughter from the little boys.) And may I add before the curtain goes up that immediately after the entertainment we want you all to file out into the Christian Endeavor room, where there will be a Christmas tree, 'with all the fixin's,' as the boys say." (Shrill whistling from the little boys and immoderate applause from everyone.)

There will then be a wait of twenty-five minutes, while sounds of hammering and dropping may be heard from behind the curtains. The Boys' Club orchestra will render the "Poet and Peasant Overture" four times in succession, each time differently.

At last one side of the curtains will be drawn back; the other will catch on something and have to be released by hand; someone will whisper loudly, "Put out the lights," following which the entire house will be plunged into darkness. Amid catcalls from the little boys, the footlights will at last go on, disclosing:

The windows in the rear of the vestry rather ineffectively concealed by a group of small fir trees on standards, one of which has already fallen over, leaving exposed a corner of the map of Palestine and the list of gold-star classes for November. In the center of the stage is a larger tree, undecorated, while at the extreme left, invisible to everyone in the audience except those sitting at the extreme right, is an imitation fireplace, leaning against the wall.

Twenty-five seconds too early little Flora Rochester will prance out from the wings, uttering the first shrill notes of a song, and will have to be grabbed by eager hands and pulled back. Twenty-four seconds later the piano will begin "The Return of the Reindeer" with a powerful accent on the first note of each bar, and Flora Rochester, Lillian McNulty, Gertrude Hamingham and Martha Wrist will swirl on, dressed in white, and advance heavily into the footlights, which will go out.

There will then be an interlude while Mr. Neff, the sexton, adjusts the connection, during which the four little girls stand undecided whether to brave it out or cry. As a compromise they giggle and are herded back into the wings by Mrs. Drury, amid applause. When the lights go on again, the applause becomes deafening, and as Mr. Neff walks triumphantly away, the little boys in the audience will whistle: "There she goes, there she goes, all dressed up in her Sunday clothes!"

"The Return of the Reindeer" will be started again and the show-girls will reappear, this time more gingerly and somewhat dispirited. They will, however, sing the following, to the music of the "Ballet Pizzicato" from "Sylvia":

"We greet you, we greet you,

On this Christmas Eve so fine.

We greet you, we greet you,

And wish you a good time."

They will then turn toward the tree and Flora Rochester will advance, hanging a silver star on one of the branches, meanwhile reciting a verse, the only distinguishable words of which are: "I am Faith so strong and pure—"

At the conclusion of her recitation, the star will fall off.

Lillian McNulty will then step forward and hang her star on a branch, reading her lines in clear tones:

"And I am Hope, a virtue great,

My gift to Christmas now I make,

That children and grown-ups may hope today

That tomorrow will be a merry Christmas Day."

The hanging of the third star will be consummated by Gertrude Hamingham, who will get as far as "Sweet Charity I bring to place upon the tree—" at which point the strain will become too great and she will forget the remainder. After several frantic glances toward the wings, from which Mrs. Drury is sending out whispered messages to the effect that the next line begins, "My message bright—" Gertrude will disappear, crying softly.

After the morale of the cast has been in some measure restored by the pianist, who, with great presence of mind, plays a few bars of "Will There Be Any Stars In My Crown?" to cover up Gertrude's exit, Martha Wrist will unleash a rope of silver tinsel from the foot of the tree, and, stringing it over the boughs as she skips around in a circle, will say, with great assurance:

"'Round and 'round the tree I go,

Through the holly and the snow

Bringing love and Christmas cheer

Through the happy year to come."

At this point there will be a great commotion and jangling of sleigh-bells off-stage, and Mr. Creamer, rather poorly disguised as Santa Claus, will emerge from the opening in the imitation fire-place. A great popular demonstration for Mr. Creamer will follow. He will then advance to the footlights, and, rubbing his pillow and ducking his knees to denote joviality, will say thickly through his false beard:

"Well, well, well, what have we here? A lot of bad little boys and girls who aren't going to get any Christmas presents this year? (Nervous laughter from the little boys and girls.) Let me see, let me see! I have a note here from Dr. Whidden. Let's see what it says. (Reads from a paper on which there is obviously nothing written.) 'If you and the young people of the Intermediate Department will come into the Christian Endeavor room, I think we may have a little surprise for you ...' Well, well, well! What do you suppose it can be? (Cries of "I know, I know!" from sophisticated ones in the audience.) Maybe it is a bottle of castor-oil! (Raucous jeers from the little boys and elaborately simulated disgust on the part of the little girls.) Well, anyway, suppose we go out and see? Now if Miss Liftnagle will oblige us with a little march on the piano, we will all form in single file—"

At this point there will ensue a stampede toward the Christian Endeavor room, in which chairs will be broken, decorations demolished, and the protesting Mr. Creamer badly hurt.

This will bring to a close the first part of the entertainment. 🕱

WAITING FOR SANTY: A CHRISTMAS PLAYLET

BY S.J. PERELMAN
(WITH A BOW TO MR. CLIFFORD ODETS)

Scene: *The sweatshop of S. Claus, a manufacturer of children's toys, on North Pole Street. Time: The night before Christmas. At rise, seven gnomes, Rankin, Panken, Rivkin, Riskin, Ruskin, Briskin, and Praskin, are discovered working furiously to fill orders piling up at stage right. The whir of lathes, the hum of motors, and the hiss of drying lacquer are so deafening that at times the dialogue cannot be heard, which is very vexing if you vex easily. (Note: the parts of Rankin, Panken, Rivkin, Riskin, Ruskin, Briskin, and Praskin are interchangeable, and may be secured directly from your dealer or the factory.)*

RISKIN (*filing a Meccano girder, bitterly*): A parasite, a leech, a blood-sucker—altogether a five-star nogoodnick! Starvation wages we get so he can ride around in red team with reindeers!

RUSKIN (*jeering*): Hey, Karl Marx, whyn'tcha hire a hall?

RISKIN (*sneering*): Scab! Stool pigeon! Company spy! (*They tangle and rain blows on each other. While waiting for these to dry, each returns to his respective task.*)

BRISKIN (*sadly, to Panken*): All day long I'm painting "Snow Queen" on these Flexible Flyers and my little Irving lays in a cold tenement with the gout.

PANKEN: You said before it was the mumps.

BRISKIN (*with a fatalistic shrug*): The mumps—the gout—go argue with City Hall.

PANKEN (*kindly, passing him a bowl*): Here, take a piece fruit.

BRISKIN (*chewing*): It ain't bad, for wax fruit.

PANKEN (*with pride*): I painted it myself.

BRISKIN (*rejecting the fruit*): Ptoo! Slave psychology!

RIVKIN (*suddenly, half to himself, half to the Party*): I got a belly full of stars, baby. You make me feel like I swallowed a Roman candle.

PRASKIN (*curiously*): What's wrong with the kid?

RISKIN: What's wrong with all of us? The system! Two years he and Claus's daughter's been making goo-goo eyes behind the old man's back.

PRASKIN: So what?

RISKIN (*scornfully*): So what? Economic determinism! What do you think the kid's name is—J. Pierpont Rivkin? He ain't even got for a bottle Dr. Brown's Celery Tonic. I tell you, it's like gall in my mouth two young people shouldn't have a room where they could make great music.

RANKIN (*warningly*): Shhh! Here she comes now! (*Stella Claus enters, carrying a portable gramophone. She and Rivkin embrace, place a record on the turntable, and begin a very slow waltz, unmindful that the gramophone is playing "Cohen on the Telephone."*)

STELLA (*dreamily*): Love me, sugar?

RIVKIN: I can't sleep, I can't eat, that's how I love you. You're a double malted with two scoops of whipped cream; you're the moon rising over Mosholu Parkway; you're a two weeks' vacation at Camp Nitgedaiget! I'd pull down the Chrysler Building to make a bobbie pin for your hair!

STELLA: I've got a stomach full of anguish. Oh, Rivvy, what'll we do?

PANKEN (*sympathetically*): Here, try a piece fruit.

RIVKIN (*fiercely*): Wax fruit—that's been my whole life! Imitations! Substitutes! Well, I'm through! Stella, tonight I'm telling your old man. He can't play mumblety-peg with two human beings! (*The tinkle of sleigh bells is heard offstage, followed by a voice shouting, "Whoa, Dasher! Whoa, Dancer!" A moment later S. Claus enters in a gust of mock snow. He is a pompous bourgeois of sixty-five who affects a white beard and a false air of benevolence. But tonight the ruddy color is missing from his cheeks, his step falters, and he moves heavily. The gnomes hastily replace the marzipan they have been filching.*)

STELLA (*anxiously*): Papa! What did the specialist say?

CLAUS (*brokenly*): The biggest professor in the country...the best cardiac man that money could buy...I tell you I was like a wild man.

STELLA: Pull yourself together, Sam!

CLAUS: It's no use. Adhesions, diabetes, sleeping sickness, decalcomania—oh, my God! I got to cut out climbing in chimneys, he says—me, Sanford Claus, the biggest toy concern in the world!

STELLA (*soothingly*): After all, it's only one man's opinion.

CLAUS: No, no, he cooked my goose. I'm like a broken uke after a Yosian picnic. Rivkin!

RIVKIN: Yes, Sam.

CLAUS: My boy, I've had my eye on you for a long time. You and Stella thought you were too foxy for an old man, didn't you? Well, let bygones be bygones. Stella, do you love this gnome?

STELLA (*simply*): He's the whole stage show at the Music Hall, Papa; he's Toscanini conducting Beethoven's Fifth; he's—

CLAUS (*curtly*): Enough already. Take him. From now on he's a partner in the firm. (*As all exclaim, Claus holds up his hand for silence.*) And tonight he can take my route and make the deliveries. It's the least I could do for my own flesh and blood. (*As the happy couple kiss, Claus wipes away a suspicious moisture and turns to the other gnomes.*) Boys, do you know what day tomorrow is?

GNOMES (*crowding around expectantly*): Christmas!

CLAUS: Correct. When you look in your envelopes tonight, you'll find a little present from me—a forty-percent pay cut. And the first one who opens his trap—gets this. (*As he holds up a tear-gas bomb and beams at them, the gnomes utter cries of joy, join hands, and dance around him shouting exultantly. All except Riskin and Briskin, that is, who exchange a quick glance and go underground.*)

CURTAIN 💀

XMAS WORDS

BY ROY BLOUNT JR.

It is at this special time of the year, and especially of this extra-special year in particular, that we realize how urgent is our need to foster love and faith and brotherhood and—at any rate faith, and by that I mean consumer confidence. When Americans, of all people, are afflicted with what the singer-songwriter Roger Miller called "shellout falter"—a reluctance to spend—then the whole world is liable, as Mr. Miller put it so well in his song "Dang Me," to "lack fourteen dollars having twenty-seven cents."

Are we going to let it be said that all we had this Christmas to cheer was cheer itself? No! Let's put the holly back in shopaholic, let's get jingle-bullish. We owe it to ourselves, to the world, and to future generations. The more presents we spring for now, the lighter the tax burden is going to be down the line.

You notice how much more merrily that last sentence bounced along because I chose *spring* to express spending, instead of, say, *plunge*; and *lighter* instead of, say, *less staggering*. Words are important. So let's say "bah, humbug" to *b*-words like *bailout* and *bankrupt*. Let's digress from anything ending in *-ession*. Let's entertain some new, upbeat holiday words.

Why not wake up tomorrow morning feeling *consumptious*? Rhymes with *scrumptious*, and approaches *sumptuous*. When we're consumptious we've got that fire in the belly that's burning a hole in our pocket. We're going to be pumping bucks today, we're going to open our hearts to goods and services, we're going to take it upon ourselves to help America, and consequently the world, *reconomize*. In so doing, we can personalize what is just about the only appealing phrase regarding the economy that has emerged this year: each of us can be his or her own *stimulus package*.

The season of giving is upon us. Need that sound like such a threat? Let's see if we can spruce up that venerable old word *generous*, which can be so cringe-inducing when we hear it spoken over the phone by a stranger calling in the interest of a charity. "I hope you will be as generous this year as last" puts us on the spot, so let's spread *generous* out. I don't think we want to go to *heterogenerous*, because people might think we're talking about sex, and there will be plenty of time for that after we get our mercantile heat back on. (For this reason, even businesses whose appeal is essentially spicy should resist, for now, the temptation to send their customers *illicitations*.) But *autogenerous*, as in *autobiographical*, might remind us that giving unto others is also giving unto ourselves, especially if others give back unto us and therefore unto themselves, and we buy our presents at their store and vice-versa. Does *auto-* strike an ominous note? Let me just say that if each of us becomes a *caregiver* this Christmas, there will be a lot more shining faces this New Year's in Detroit. And Japan.

Let us not shrink from taking a look at the word *Christmas*. It's a fine old word and I for one would be loath to suggest that it has lost its edge entirely. But it doesn't exactly sing. The only thing it rhymes with is *isthmus*, and that but loosely. How do you like the sound of *Jingle Day*? Says bells and sunshine, says catchy marketing, says plenty of change. The rhymes sell themselves: *mingle, tingle, Kringle, Pringles, bling'll,* and *hey, sleigh, pray, pay, hooray.* We might even go a little more on-the-nose: *Ka-chingleday.*

And incidentally, when you take your tree down and put your ornaments away for next year (yes, of course there will be a next year, don't even ask such a question), do you know the best way to protect those ornaments? By wrapping them in newspaper. Several sheets per ornament. Maybe a whole newspaper section per ornament. And magazines and books are good to put between wrapped ornaments for further protection. Not to knock the tissue-paper industry, but what has it ever done for, say, people who support themselves and their families (not to mention the Jingle Day puppies their families have been promised) by thinking up words? ☻

CHRISTMAS CAROL

BY LEWIS LAPHAM

You can tell the ideals of a nation by its advertisements.
—NORMAN DOUGLAS

𝕎𝖆𝖓𝖉𝖊𝖗𝖎𝖓𝖌 among the remote shelves of a Fifth Avenue bookstore in late October, I came across a small stack of books on the floor near a freight elevator, ten or twelve copies of a cheaply printed paperback bound up with string and marked with a slip of paper identifying them as goods in transit. Assuming that they were what was left of the summer's best-selling news about the O.J. Simpson trial, and curious to see which authors and what theories of criminal justice were being returned to pulp, I lifted the corner of the invoice and was surprised to find Charles Dickens's *A Christmas Carol* in a red cover with the familiar illustration of Mr. Fezziwig's ball. I had mistaken the direction of the shipment. Books that I had thought were going out were coming in, but the sales clerks apparently hadn't decided where to place what the publisher's tag line described as "the most beloved Christmas tale of them all."

As I continued to browse among the season's newest political tracts, many of them about bringing discipline to the nation's economy and strengthening its penal codes, it occurred to me that maybe the clerks were embarrassed by the mawkish sentimentality of the beloved tale. Maybe they were reluctant to display it in the front of a store that undoubtedly numbered among its patrons quite a few corporate managers apt to possess precisely those qualities that Dickens so deplored in Ebenezer Scrooge—"Hard and sharp as flint, from which no steel had ever struck out generous fire, secret, and self-contained, and solitary as an oyster." It won't do these days to make a mockery of wealth or portray a rich businessman as anything other than a hero of the people. Money is the proof of grace, and a miser, as every schoolchild knows, is a great and good conservative. The plotline of *A Christmas Carol* didn't fit the bracing spirit of the times, and neither did its irresponsible moral lesson. Here was old Scrooge, an exemplary Republican, troubled in his sleep by ghostly dreams of human kindness, changed into a gibbering liberal at the sight of a crippled child. Hardly an inspiring tale of triumphant profit-taking and certainly not one that anybody would want to place next to a handsome photograph of Newt Gingrich or Peter Lynch.

Sensitive to the predicament of the sales staff, I wondered whether it might be possible to rewrite *A Christmas Carol* in a way that more nearly matched the forthright, manly teaching of the Contract with America. Not an easy revision, of course, and one that would require some fairly heavy-handed deconstruction of the text, but after a few moments' thought, and taking heart from the brisk sales at the cash register of *Beyond Prozac* and *Your Sacred Self*, I understood that the tale was probably best retold as a sequel. As follows:

STAVE I

Our story begins with the appalling sight of Ebenezer T. Scrooge V, a benign and mild-mannered man in his late fifties, generous to a fault, who for many years has been squandering his great-great-grandfather's noble fortune on misguided schemes to rescue the unrepentant poor. The imbecile philanthropist sits reading a romantic novel by Leo Tolstoy in a small but cheerful library surrounded by the worthless tokens of an idealist's misspent life—photographs signed by Mahatma Gandhi, Gary Hart, and Hillary Clinton, civic awards mounted in second-rate silver, a pet owl, forgotten reports from forgotten presidential commissions appointed to study racial injustice and environmental disgrace, Mark

Twain's walking stick, books published by Marxist university professors, framed letters of appreciation from the students of an elementary school in Ciudad Juárez, a bowl of Hudson River mud.

It is the hour after sunset on Christmas Eve, and the rest of the house is full of music and light. The children and grandchildren of Ebenezer Scrooge V, all of them too careless with money (too careless by far) and too easily moved to laughter (to the point of impertinence), have invited so many guests to dinner that they can't remember how many places to set at the table. They make a joyful noise of their preparations, the clattering of plates and the popping of champagne corks joined with the sound of a piano and three voices singing "God Rest Ye Merry Gentlemen."

The ghost of Jacob Marley drifts through the library door looking as dismal as it looked in London in 1843, "like a bad lobster in a dark cellar," but instead of being weighted down with heavy locks and chains, the apparition takes the form of a scolding family lawyer come to correct the spendthrift heir with the switch of sound advice. Scrooge suggests a glass of wine, "a little something to restore the color to your cheeks," but Marley waves the offer impatiently aside and reminds the descendant of his former partner that the money is all but gone, the trust funds nearly exhausted, and the warehouses on the verge of bankruptcy. Before floating out the window, the ghost tells Scrooge to expect three unearthly visitors, three spirits who, if he heeds them well, will recall him to the bosom of Mammon.

STAVE II

The Ghost of Christmas Past bears a remarkable resemblance to John D. Rockefeller, the founder of the fortune of that name and known during his long and grasping life as the incarnation of stinginess. Somber as a pallbearer, looking more like a starved New England clergyman than a well-fed financier, the ghost bids Scrooge rise from his chair and walk with him in the night sky on a grand tour of America as it existed a hundred years ago, the old, economically competitive America, innocent of labor unions and free of feminists. The spirit shows Scrooge a series of canonical scenes: gangs of Chinese laborers laying railroad track across the Nevada desert, handsome policeman mounted on thoroughbred horses suppressing Irish mobs, criminals on treadmills, unheated shoe factories in the dead of winter, the children bent to their tasks in orderly and uncomplaining rows, patriotic newspapermen wearing checked suits and bowler hats, bowing like Kewpie dolls to the magnates of the Gilded Age, grim country parsons singing psalms, picturesque beggars in sprightly rags, indigent pensioners dying as unobtrusively as flies, too proud of their American heritage (independent and self-reliant) to bother anybody with a plea for help or a cry of pain.

Presented as an album of prints by Currier & Ives, the little scenes blink on and off at regular intervals through the scudding cloud, and to each of them the Ghost of Christmas Past affixes, like a Christmas ribbon or a sprig of holly, the ornament of an edifying thought:

"Beware, Ebenezer Scrooge, the ageless ingratitude of the poor."

"Never show sympathy to people from whom you can expect nothing in return."

"Charity destroys initiative and rots the will to industry and enterprise."

Scrooge stands abashed before the solemn images of frugality and thrift. For the first time in his wastrel's life, he begins to apprehend the majesty of a cold and savage heart, and when the spirit returns him to the comfort of his library he glances at the fire burning on the hearth and thinks that it would cast a purer light with one log instead of four.

STAVE III

No sooner has the clock struck the hour of ten than the Ghost of Christmas Present rises up through the floor like the genie from Aladdin's Lamp—a figure not dissimilar to that of Rush Limbaugh or Roseanne—grinning, corpulent, and huge, the soul of perfect selfishness. Dressed in a loose gown of flowered silk and wearing on its gigantic head a crown of cloves

and pineapples, the apparition claps Scrooge boisterously on the back
and announces, amid gusts of booming laughter, that it has come to
teach the lessons of gratified desire. Only fools and saints and New Deal
Democrats subordinate their own comforts to those of others or put off
until tomorrow pleasures that can be seized today. So saying, and as if
to prove its point, the great spirit seizes Scrooge by the wrist, drags him
upward through the roof, and spreads before him a second panoramic
view of America the Beautiful. Once again the purpose is didactic, but
instead of dwelling on the triumphs of the past, the genie of the shopper's lamp displays the glories of the miraculous present. The settings
are all suburban—office parks and shopping malls, resort communities
protected by high walls and iron gates, ski lodges, university quadrangles,
boat marinas. No black or brown people appear anywhere in sight—no
red or yellow people, nobody wearing rings in his ear or her nose, no
loud musical instruments, no government bureaucrats, no street ven-
dors selling filthy foreign foods. All the factories have been turned into
overpriced restaurants, all the assembly lines neatly trimmed and down-
sized (like the hedges at the entrance of a good hotel), all the IRS agents
turned into tennis instructors or personal trainers.

Enfolding Scrooge within the giant arc of its ham-like arm, and with
a chuckle as merry as the holiday catalogue from Bloomingdale's, the
Ghost of Christmas Present invites him to gaze upon the prizes that
money buys for people mature enough to know that in the end and
when all is said and done (no matter what happens to anybody in Bosnia
or Queens), they have only themselves to please. From the depths of
the now starry night a magnificent procession of shining luxuries floats
before Scrooge's eyes, and as the objects pass splendidly by, the great
spirit names them as the orphaned pleasures that Scrooge has foolishly
forsworn.

The last yacht and the last cashmere cap drift slowly away to the
south, and Scrooge once again discovers himself in his library listlessly

turning the pages of a book that suddenly seems dingy and old as Leo Tolstoy's beard. It occurs to him that maybe he has lived too long in the company of the dispossessed. As a child he had known about the marble fountains and the heavy motor cars, and he had seen magazine advertisements for the racehorses and Italian suits, but the second unearthly visitor had surprised him with some of the newer and more complicated toys—menageries of tame politicians in silver cages, miniature billionaires no bigger than fawns, newspaper editors cleverly contrived to sing like the golden, mechanical birds once made for the amusement of Oriental princes.

STAVE IV

In the hour before midnight the Spirit of Christmas Yet to Come, an ominous and silent figure in a black shroud, summons Scrooge with the gesture of one outstretched hand—a hand as pale as death—to the French doors leading out into the rose garden. Scrooge has by now become wary of strange sights. Guessing at the nature of the dreadful entertainment likely to appear among the rosebushes, he rises unwillingly from his chair, afraid to look upon the face of doom. In a small and creeping voice he asks for program notes: "You are about to show me shadows of things that have not happened but will happen in the time before us? Is that so, Spirit?"

The phantom neither speaks nor moves. The outstretched hand draws back the curtain of the night, and the garden blooms with scenes of pandemonium that look like they might have been jointly painted by Jan Brueghel and Hieronymus Bosch: the entire population of Oklahoma stoned on drugs and heavy metal rock bands loose in the Iowa corn, undocumented aliens disembarking from ships (like the animals descending from Noah's ark) in every port on the once well-defended American coast, unemployed corporate executives (white and middle-aged) selling apples on the steps of the Pentagon, lewd women (as young and licentious as Calvin Klein's child models, as old and insatiable as the Wife of Bath) selling sexual favors in Harvard Yard, gay and lesbian parades in Salt Lake City, debates in Congress conducted in gangsta rap, fifth-grade classrooms studying the history of pornographic film (a twenty-seven-part series produced by the Public Broadcasting System and narrated by Bill Moyers), shiftless fathers throwing away their children like empty beer cans, unwed mothers nursing unbaptised infants on the floor of the New York Stock Exchange, altar boys spinning roulette wheels and nobody reading William Bennett's *Book of Virtues*, young black men in velvet top hats standing around on street corners frightening the police.

Scrooge cannot bear to look upon the dreadful scene for more than twenty minutes. He falls trembling to his knees, clutching at the phantom's robe. "Hear me, good Spirit. Why show me this if I am past all hope? I am not the man I was. I will not be the man I must have been but for this gift of Phil Gramm's grace."

The phantom departs as silently as it came, and the exhausted Scrooge falls into a fitful sleep, dreaming of reform schools.

STAVE V

Faithful to the miracle of redemption, Scrooge awakens on Christmas morning restored to the winter glory of his ancestors—his cheeks noticeably shriveled, his blood four degrees colder in his stiffened veins, a suddenly squeezing, wrenching, envious man whose movements have become as quick and nervous as a lizard's tongue. At last Scrooge has come to know the meaning of a dollar and the beauty of the bottom line. In a hurry to be up and dressed, his hands busy with his shirt and tie while at the same time talking on a cellular phone, he cancels the clown ordered for a children's cancer ward, instructs his brokers to buy shares in companies that own and manage prisons, orders the closing of seven factories, chases out of the house the company of useless guests, berates the cook (for putting too much stuffing in the Christmas turkey),

disinherits his grandchildren, and sells the owl. Later in the morning, on his way to his office in New York City, Scrooge walks briskly
north on Fifth Avenue, shaking his shrunken fists at the Christmas
wreaths but coveting, like any other loyal American, all the precious
merchandise in all the better stores. Asked for money at the corner
of Fifty-seventh Street by a crippled child as surely doomed as Tiny
Tim Cratchit, Scrooge rebukes the waif for his insolence and kicks
away its crutch.

TWO SELECTIONS FROM I HATE CHRISTMAS

BY DANIEL BLYTHE

1. **The** *Best Ways to Deal with Carol-Singers*
(In ascending order of probable effectiveness.)

- Have a sign on your door saying "No Carol-Singers."

- Have a sign on your door saying "Carol-Singers Must Die."

- Have the television on very loudly.

- Draw the curtains, turn off the lights and pretend to be out.

- Stand at the windows wearing dark glasses and a hearing aid.

- Tell them you are a Jehovah's Witness and therefore don't celebrate Christmas.

- Pretend to be a foreigner who has never heard of Christmas.

- Ask *them* for money.

- Say "Little boys, little girls, I can smell you! Come on in!" in your best Child Catcher voice.

- Say you don't have any money, but you can pay them in last year's brazil nuts.

- Come to the front door naked.

- Come to the front door wiping a kitchen knife on a bloodstained apron, and then invite them in.

- Set up water-cannon turrets linked to a tap inside the house, with which you can spray them with icy jets as soon as they start to sing.

- Come to the door looking wildly up and down the street, tearing at your hair and rolling your eyes, and saying,"The voices! The voices! They're back again!"

- Set up a tape playing some evil-sounding backwards Latin and stentorian laughter, which goes off at the same time as an array of green lights and swirling dry ice. Then answer the door dressed as Death, complete with scythe.

2. **Be** *Careful Out There*

(Here are some more thoughts about the kinds of mishaps which might well befall you over the festive season. Take care now.)

- Just before Christmas 2004, Playtex, the makers of the **Wonderbra**, recalled their "Deep Plunge Deeply Daring" model, designed for plunging necklines, when it was discovered that the strap could easily snap. (Presumably thousands of men then rushed out to buy one for their wives before they vanished from the shelves.)

- "People think **fairy lights** last forever—they don't, and can kill. They get crumpled and heaped into the attic for the rest of the year. Wires get bent, frayed and knotted and can all too easily lead to electrocution,' says RoSPA Safety Advisor David Jenkins. Apparently 12 percent of Christmas injuries—mainly burns and electric shocks—are caused by fairy lights.

- **Candles** are another source of danger. David Jenkins from RoSPA is back again: "Candles are popular gifts at the moment, but they pose a major threat. They should never be left unattended or near anything that can catch fire, like curtains or decorations." (Presumably Mr. Jenkins added that you should also avoid sitting in the middle of the road during rush-hour, that it might be inadvisable to file your nails with a kitchen knife, and that it can be silly to stand on top of a hill during a storm brandishing a wet sword and shouting, "Thunder-gods, do your worst!")

- Meanwhile, 41 per cent of Christmas accidents are caused by people falling off chairs, tables and ladders while putting up **decorations**. These injuries could be reduced to zero by the simple act of not putting up decorations.

- And then there are the specific dangers of **tinsel**. Chipping Sodbury school in Gloucestershire banned the wearing of tinsel on its non-uniform day in 2004 because of the health and safety dangers. Deputy headteacher Mel Jeffries said: "We want our children to enjoy Christmas and have a good time, but at the same time making sure there are no accidents to spoil it. If tinsel is worn loosely around the neck it can be pulled tight and we don't want anything like that." Let's hope nobody tried to throttle anyone with a deadly tie once they got back into uniform.

- Don't forget **wrapping**. Ribbons and string can cause problems for cats. That's problems as in making them choke to death if they get hold of them.

- Lighting the **Christmas pudding** can result in a nasty "flashback" effect—no, nothing to do with suddenly remembering the awful thing which Uncle Frank said to Aunt Bethan over the sprouts in 1995. This is caused by people continuing to pour brandy onto the pudding once the match is lit.

- **Trees** are responsible for approximately 34 per cent of Christmas accidents: those on offer include being poked in the eye by branches, back-strain from lifting the thing into the house, scratches from foliage and cuts caused by inexpert attempts at pruning. It sounds like

the stuff of a bad sci-fi novel, but 2,000 people a year are attacked by
their Christmas trees.

- And while we're at it, let's mention some odd stuff called "**Prolong**,"
  which you can spray on your pine tree to stop it shedding. Or maybe
  you'd better not. If you ingest the stuff, a safety campaign warns,
  it can cause diarrhea and vomiting. (One sometimes has to wonder who these safety campaigns are aimed at. You do know you're
  not supposed to drink bleach either, right? And that jumping off tall
  buildings is dangerous?)

- While we're on the subject of **foliage**—the Christmas cherry is a
  popular houseplant, but its unripened orange berries can cause
  stomach pains. The Christmas rose, sometimes called the snow or
  winter rose, is toxic if eaten in large quantities—apparently it's such
  an effective cause of diarrhea that it was used as a purgative by the
  ancient Greeks. The seer Melampus used the plant to cure the mad-
  ness of King Proteus' daughters, who had become convinced that
  they were cows.

- Taking a heavy **turkey** out of the oven can cause a condition known
  as "turkey-lifter's back." Presumably one is meant to observe the
  technique of Russian weightlifters at the Olympics before attempting such a feat.

- **Alcohol** is the most common source of Christmas ailments and
  injuries. It's plentiful at Christmas, of course, and everybody gets in
  far more than they need. There will always be the assumption that
  people want to sample stuff which they wouldn't touch with a barge-
  pole at any other time of the year, such as Harvey's Bristol Cream
  or Kahlúa, and this will lead to swift inebriation and some unfortu-
  nate incidents. The festive tipple is responsible for everything from

punch-ups at the office party to aggravating depression and bringing about surprise pregnancies. (On the other hand, wasn't it one of the latter which started the whole Christmas thing off?)

- The party season can sometimes cause **deafness**, warns the Royal National Institute for the Deaf. (I said, "THE PARTY SEASON CAN SOMETIMES . . ." Ahem.) Dance floor noise can reach 110 decibels, which is the equivalent of the levels produced by a jet engine. The RNID advice for those going out to clubs and gigs over the festive season is to stand well away from the speakers, take regular breaks and consider wearing earplugs. (This is especially advisable if you're thinking of attending a Mariah Carey concert.)

- And don't forget the danger of being blinded by houses bedecked with dazzling Stars of Bethlehem and streams of "icicle-effect" lights—or of your children being scared to death by evil, dark-eyed fiberglass Santas flashing on and off. ☠

THE TERRIBLE FOURTH DAY OF CHRISTMAS

BY SCOTT HORTON

$\mathfrak{It}$ seems that in most households in America where Christmas is celebrated, it occurs on December 25, and the tree is stripped and ready to be hauled off by the garbage men the following weekend. December 26, of course, is the day for the return of unwanted gifts. This marks Christmas celebrated as consumerism; a justification for boosted retail sales.

For centuries before the commercialization of Christmas, however, it was a spiritual holiday that was anticipated for the four preceding Sundays of Advent, and then it was followed by eleven further days, ending on January 6. Each of those days had a specific significance in terms of the liturgical calendar, and popular customs also arose with respect to them, of which the Twelfth Night might be the most significant in the English-speaking world, a day for revels. But alas, none of this could be successfully converted to a rite of consumerism (and anyway, the urge was to get all those accounts settled and sales booked by year's end), so it all seems to be fading away.

Today, the fourth day of Christmas, is the Feast of the Holy Innocents, or in the older English usage, Childermas. Most Americans only have a vague understanding of what it's about. King Herod, we learn in Matthew 2:16, ordered that all infant males in Bethlehem be put to death. He was apparently inspired by word of the approach of the three magi, seeking an infant king in that city, and fearful of a plot against his throne. The story does not appear in any other gospel text, nor in any contemporaneous history, which causes many historians to express skepticism about it.

Nevertheless, the commemoration of this horrible act of slaughter was incorporated into the Christmas season, and it evolved a number of traditions. In the Middle Ages it figured in Christmas pageants, especially a famous one in Coventry, surrounded by what may be the most hauntingly beautiful of the English carols—dating to the sixteenth century at least—the Coventry Carol. It also figured in some cruel practices in England—as histories of the Coventry Carol note that this day was one on which children were whipped to remind them to be mournful.

This hardly fits into modern celebrations which focus only on the uplifting notes of the religious tradition, leaving those seemingly more cruel behind. What purpose can be found for this commemoration today? It interjects cruelty and inhumanity at a time which should be marked by peace and festivity. Some modern Christian writers try to transform the incident into a polemic against abortion. But of course, the legend does not speak to the unborn, and this understanding has no historical basis.

I have a different understanding of this story and its function in the Christmas cycle. We think of course of the innocent children. But the actor in this story is King Herod the Great, a figure with a disputed historical legacy, but certainly attached to much cruelty. This story is a reminder of the tendency of those who hold temporal power to engage in corrupt deeds, even horrific crimes, to retain that power. Christ of course made no claim on Herod's crown, nor did he challenge the rule of the Romans. But in the thinking of the legend of the innocents, even the suggestion of an alternate authority was unbearable to Herod, an unrighteous ruler. The martyrdom of the innocents reminds us of this all too human failing. It reminds us never to repose too much trust and faith in those who hold temporal power, and not to confuse their acts with justice. In the end justice must be understood divorced from the power and ambitions of individual political figures, who being only human will, as Albertus Magnus reminds us, often stray from the path of righteousness.

Otherwise, of course, you can just associate the fourth day of Christmas with four calling birds—which makes much less fuss. 💀

SELECTIONS FROM MERCURIUS RELIGIOSUS: FAITHFULLY COMMUNICATING TO THE WHOLE NATION, THE VANITY OF CHRISTMAS

BY ANONYMOUS

I. **The** Observation of this Feast hath no warrant in the holy Scriptures, for we cannot find that it was ever commanded or practiced, either by Christ himself, his Apostles, or Apostolicall men ... God himself hath appointed a day in remembrance of his Son's Birth, Death, Resurrection, and all that concerns him, which is the First day of the week commonly known by the name of the Lord's Day; Inasmuch then as the Lord hath appointed a time for that purpose, it can be no less then high presumption ... when we add to his Ordinances, or set up any invention of our own, with his Institutions: Whereof this Feast of Christmas seems to be guilty, for that it doth upon the matter imply, that the day which God ordained for the memorial of Christ was not sufficient, unless we should add another, or a fitter time than God's, making ourselves wiser than God in this matter.

II. We know not the Day, nor at what time of the year Christ was born, so that we are very blindly led in setting our devotion so punctually upon the 25 of *December*; for neither the Scripture nor any authentic human writer, do give us the least assurance that this was the day or about the time of his Nativity: The Lord perhaps, purposely concealing the day of his Son's Birth, to prevent the Idolizing of it ... yea it may be further said, that in all probability our Savior was not born on that day, nor at that season of the year, but rather in the Summer time, for tis not likely that the people should be called to travel from all parts of *Judea*, to the chief Cities of their Tribes, in the depth of Winter; nor that the Shepherds could keep the field by night with their flocks at that season of the year ...

III. This Feast of Christmas was devised by our superstitious Ancestors in meet imitation of the Pagans and Heathenish people who had a festival called *Saturnalia*, or *Bacchanalia*, consisting of twelve days, dedicated to those imaginary Idol Gods, *Saturn* and *Bacchus*, which were spent in games and revellings, but colored over with the pretence of Devotion and Sacrificing to those Deities ... Tis most certain that the time of our Christmas Festival is the same with theirs, for as they kept six days of the old year, and six days of the new year so do we, and as they spent those twelve days in Riot, Excess, and gaming, so do we; and as they pretended Religion and Piety to their God *Bacchus* or *Saturn*, in the observation of those days, so do we pretend Devotion to the memory of our Savior Christ in the keeping of them, so that upon the matter there is nothing changed but the name of this Feast, from what it was in the days of Paganism.

IV. The vanity of observing this Festival may further appear by the quality of those persons and people who are so zealously addicted to the observation of it, and plead so strongly for it, if we mind them well, we shall find them to be none of the best, nor to be guilty of over-much knowledge or piety ... It is no wonder then that so many papish, ignorant, idle, deboyst, superstitious, Atheistical, loose, and profane people, are unwilling to part with Christmas, it being a time so suitable to their corrupt humors, and base lusts.

V. Consider, that although piety is pretended, yet all manner of profaneness is practiced these twelve days, Custom hath made Christmas a time of Licentious Liberty, for all sorts of persons, as if the remembrance of the grace of God which hath abounded in the gift of Jesus Christ, gave toleration for men to abound in Sin and Wickedness, Gluttony, Drunkenness, Chambering, Wantonness, Riot, Excess, Carding & Dicing, are counted not only lawful, but commendable in Christmas, as if by such doings Christ were honored, and took delight in these works of darkness ... It is very strange that in these days of the Gospel, the Devil should so delude Christians, as to make them do him service, and yet make them believe that they serve Christ . . . For of all the whole year, this time (though set apart for Christ) hath proved the Devil's best harvest.

VI. . . . Doubtless the Lord will one day say to the best observers of this time of Christmas, *Who hath required this of you?* In what part of my Word have you found any command or rule for so doing?

But much more will he expostulate with others of the profaner sort, and will say to them, Who gave you this liberty to turn my grace into lasciviousness? Why do you celebrate my Son's Nativity with the excess of Riot? By what warrant do you spend these days and nights so contrary to my Commandments?

VII. Seventhly and lastly, the Vanity of this feast may further appear, in that it is almost utterly abolished in all Christian Reformed Churches (but ours) which upon the breaking forth of the light of the Gospel, have abandoned the gross abuses of this time, as an Heathenish Antichristian practice, becoming none but the children of darkness.

Objections for keeping Christmas, Answered.

1 Ob. This day and the other Holy days in the Twelftide is solemnized in memorial of our Savior's Nativity, and the rest in honor of the other Saints, to whose names those days are dedicated.

Ans. 1. We know not that Christ was born on this day.

2. It is more likely that our Savior was born in Summer.

3. We have neither precept nor practice from Christ or his apostles, for the keeping of this day.

4. The Sabbath was changed from the seventh day to the first day of the week, in memorial of Christ and his benefits, and is therefore called the Lord's Day.

5. New-year's-day is meetly heathenish, and so are the customs belonging to it.

6. The other days were instituted by the Popes of *Rome*, when Antichristian darkness overspread the face of the earth.

7. This Feast, pretended for the Honor of Christ, and other Saints, yields more dishonor to Christ and Christianity, than the whole year besides.

2 Ob. The observation of Christmas is of great Antiquity, and hath been continued in the Church for many ages.

Ans. 1. The Pope's Calendar is the first Record we have of this Festival; Augustine's and Christostom's Nativity Sermons are adulterate, and foisted into their Works.

2. Antiquity without other Authority is no safe rule for Christians to walk by: Superstition, Idolatry, Bigamy, &c. are ancienter then Christmas, yet not tolerable, because they can plead prescription.

3 Ob. Many learned Bishops, and other eminent men for parts and piety, have observed this Feast, as by their preaching upon it, and pleading for it, appears.

Ans. 1. Some good Ministers have used to preach upon these days to keep their people out of worse employment.

2. It is no new thing for Bishops and other learned men, to be maintainers of superstition and profanity.

3. The Scribes and Pharisees were eminent amongst the people, yet Christ nailed them up for Counterfeits.

4. Godly men may be dim-sighted in some things: *Bernardus non vidit omnia.*

4 Ob. Almost all men plead for Christmas, and it is kept by a general consent, none dissenting but a few factious precise people.

Ans. 1. We must not follow a multitude to do evil...

2. If most voices might carry things, we should have a mad world...

3. Those few that dislike the superstition and vanities of this Festival, will be found to out-weigh the giddy ignorant multitude, in point of understanding and piety.

5 Ob. The long continued custom of observing Christmas may plead for the continuance of it still.

Ans. 1. Bad customs ought rather to be broken then kept...

6 Ob. Tis a time for feasting, and entertainment of neighbors, and of giving relief and doles to poor people.

Ans. 1. Hang the Devil if he have not one trick or other to cheat the world withal.

2. Any other time of the year, is as good for that purpose as this.

3. The usual way of relieving the poor at this time, is, I fear, more out of custom and ostentation, then out of charity and true Devotion.

7. *Ob. Though some have abused this time, as the best things are liable to abusing; yet the abuse of a thing ought not to take away the use.*

*Ans.*1. This rule holds only things that are in their own nature lawful and necessary.

2. This festival is in itself unnecessary, and unlawful, because without warrant, and the world may very well spare it, and therefore being so extremely abused, it may and ought to be utterly abolished.

Exhortations

1. To the Honourable Court of Parliament, that they would cause this Romish Idol to be ground to powder, and that they would abstain from committing whoredom with it themselves.

2. To the Reverend Assembly of Divines, that they would do something before they part, towards the stigmatizing of this Pagan-Popish Strumpet…

3. To the royal city of *London*, that they would banish this grand Impostor, out of the lines of communication that the light of the Gospel may no longer be blemished with the works of Antichristian darkness.

4. To all the Clergy of this Nation, that they would no longer give countenance to this ungospel-like foolery, but set themselves to cry it down as a reproach to Christianity, though it be with the loss of some new-year's gifts, and a few customary Christmas dinners.

5. To the two famous Universities: that they would expel this youth-corrupting master of misrule out of their Colleges, no matter though the Cook and Butler grumble at it, or the Scholars miss their exceedings for that time.

6. To the Magistrates of *England*, that they would bind this unruly time of Christmas to the good behavior, or send it away with a passport to *Rome* the place of his birth.

7. To the Gentry of this Nation: that they would shut their doors against this misbegotten Epicure, and not suffer themselves and estates to be abused any longer for fashion sake, nor let their houses be polluted with the Devil's sacrifices.

8. To Almanac makers, that they would leave lying, and either find out the true time of Christ's Nativity, or blot it out of their books.

9. To all the people of this Nation, that they would dote no longer upon this *Babilonish* Hag, which hath so long enchanted them with her devout looks, pleasing pastime, and good cheer.

Written by him that loves a Choller of Brawne, and a Mince-pye, as well as any Common-Councell man in this City, 1651 💀

CHRISTMAS SHOPPING: A SURVIVOR'S GUIDE

BY DAVE BARRY

Once again, we come to the Holiday Season, a deeply religious time that each of us observes, in his own way, by going to the mall of his choice.

In the old days, it was not called the Holiday Season; the Christians called it "Christmas" and went to church; the Jews called it "Hanukkah" and went to synagogue; the atheists went to parties and drank. People passing each other on the street would say "Merry Christmas!" or "Happy Hanukkah!" or (to the atheists) "Look out for the wall!"

These days, people say "Season's Greetings," which, when you think about it, means nothing. It's like walking up to somebody and saying "Appropriate Remark" in a loud, cheerful voice. But "Season's Greetings" is safer, because it does not refer to any actual religion. Some day, I imagine, even "Season's Greetings" will be considered too religious, and we'll celebrate the Holiday Season by saying "Have a nice day."

Some of you may be unhappy with this dereligionizing of the Holiday Season, and you may have decided that, this year, you're going to celebrate it the old-fashioned way, with your family sitting around stringing cranberries and exchanging humble, handmade gifts, like on *The Waltons*. Well, you can forget it. If everybody pulled that kind of subversive stunt, the economy would collapse overnight. The government would have to intervene: It would form a cabinet-level Department of Holiday Gift-Giving, which would spend billions and billions of tax dollars to buy Barbie dolls and electronic games, which it would drop on the populace from Air Force jets, killing and maiming thousands. So, for the good of the nation, you should go along with the Holiday Program. This means you should get a large sum of money and go to a mall.

Unless you live in Indonesia, there should be several malls within five miles of your home. It makes no difference whatsoever which one you go to: Under federal law, all malls in the United States must have the same forty two chain stores. You have your chain bookstores, your chain clothing stores, your chain shoe stores, your chain restrooms, your chain electronic-game arcades.

The basic idea behind malls is that they are more convenient than cities. Cities contain streets, which are dangerous and crowded and difficult to park in. Malls, on the other hand, have parking lots, which are also dangerous and crowded and difficult to park in, but—here is the big difference—in mall parking lots, THERE ARE NO RULES. You're allowed to do anything. You can drive as fast as you want in any direction you want. I was once driving in a mall parking lot when my car was struck by a pickup truck being driven backward by a squat man with a tattoo that said "Charlie" on his forearm, who got out and explained to me, in great detail, why the accident was my fault, his reasoning being that he was violent and muscular, whereas I was neither. This kind of reasoning is legally valid in mall parking lots.

So when you get to the mall for your holiday shopping, the first thing to remember is that you should not park in the parking lot and walk to the mall buildings, because you will probably get killed. Instead, drive your car right up to and, if possible, right into, the mall building. This is perfectly legal; people do it all the time. In almost every mall I've ever been to, the corridors were littered with cars, recreational vehicles, snowmobiles and motorboats left by smart parkers.

Once you're safely in the mall, you should tie your children to you with ropes so the other shoppers won't try to buy them. Holiday shoppers have been whipped into a frenzy by months of holiday advertisements, and they will buy anything small enough to stuff into a shopping bag. If your children object to being tied, threaten to take them to see Santa Claus; that ought to shut them up.

Now you're ready for the actual shopping. Your goal should be to get it over with as quickly as possible, because the longer you stay in the mall, the longer your children will have to listen to holiday songs on the mall public-address system, and many of these songs can damage children emotionally. For example: "Frosty the Snowman" is about a snowman who befriends some children, plays with them until they learn to love him, then melts. And "Rudolph the Red-Nosed Reindeer" is about a young reindeer who, because of a physical deformity, is treated as an outcast by the other reindeer. Then along comes good, old Santa. Does he ignore the deformity? Does he look past Rudolph's nose and respect Rudolph for the sensitive reindeer he is underneath? No. Santa asks Rudolph to guide his sleigh, as if Rudolph were nothing more than some kind of headlight with legs and a tail. So unless you want your children exposed to this kind of insensitivity, you should shop quickly.

Here is a very efficient shopping method: Divide the amount of money you have by the number of people on your gift list to get an average dollar amount per person. So if you have $160, and you want to buy gifts for 10 people, your average is $16 per person. Now find something that costs $16, and buy 10 of whatever it is. You'll find many useful gifts in this price range; for example, you could get 10 family-sized bottles of vitamin B. Everyone, young and old alike, can use vitamin B, and your children are sure to shriek with delight when they find it under the tree.

If you want to buy gifts that are a little more personal, you should follow these guidelines:

Gifts for Men

Men are amused by almost any idiot thing—that is why professional ice hockey is so popular—so buying gifts for them is easy. But you should never buy them clothes. Men believe they already have all the clothes they will ever need, and new ones make them nervous. For example, your average man has 84 ties, but he wears, at most, only three of them. He has learned, through humiliating trial and error, that if he wears any of the other 81 ties, his wife will probably laugh at him ("You're not going to wear THAT tie with that suit, are you?"). So he has narrowed it down to three safe ties, and has gone several years without being laughed at. If you give him a new tie, he will pretend to like it, but deep inside he will hate you.

If you want to give a man something practical, consider tires. More than once, I would have gladly traded all the gifts I got for a new set of tires.

Gifts for Women

Again, you should avoid buying clothes, but not because women don't like clothes. The problem is sizes. First of all, women's clothing sizes don't mean anything. Suppose you're looking at a dress, and the tag says it's a size 14. You could measure that dress with every known measuring instrument, checking for every known unit of measurement, and you would never find any dimension that was 14 anythings long. Not only that, but you would never find any dimension that corresponded to the same dimension on any other size-14 dress. Not only that, but chances are you would never find any woman in the entire world who would admit to being a size 14.

Another problem is color. Women do not see color the way men do. Suppose several women are in a paint store, looking at a sample of orange paint. The paint-can label may say "orange," and the paint may appear obviously orange to a male, but the women will never use the word "orange" to describe it. They will say things like: "It has a lot of blue" or "It's much too gray." Don't ask me to explain it. All I know is, if a woman tells a man she'd like a green scarf for Christmas, he'll go out and buy a scarf that he believes to be green, based on his concept of "green," which he got from crayons in the second grade. She will look at the scarf as if it were covered with maggots, then show it to her friends and say: "I asked Harold for a green scarf, and just look at what he got me." They'll all have a good laugh, and she'll return it.

So the safest gifts for women are expensive little bottles of colorless liquids, which are sold at cosmetic counters under names such as "Eau de Water" and "Endless Night of Heavy Petting."

Gifts for Children

This is easy. You never have to figure out what to get for children, because they will tell you exactly what they want. They spend months and months researching these kinds of things by watching Saturday-morning cartoon-show advertisements. Make sure you get your children exactly what they ask for, even if you disapprove of their choices. If your child thinks he wants Murderous Bob, the Doll with the Face You Can Rip Right Off, you'd better get it. You may be worried that it might help to encourage your child's antisocial tendencies, but believe me, you have not seen antisocial tendencies until you've seen a child who is convinced that he or she did not get the right gift. 💀

SANTA RESPONDS

BY SANTA CLAUS

Dear Santa Clause,

I think that I have been very bad this year. Do you want to know some things I did? O.K. I'll tell you anyway. First of all, I have been planning to dominate the world. I've done other bad things also. That is the worst. Now, I will name some things that you will get me (or else). I want a giant machine gun to blow up the world with. I want a big evil Barbie doll. I want my own elf. If I don't get these then I will be extremely mad. So mad that I will blow up the world anyway. So Santa Clause, the world is doomed no matter what.

Hugs and Kisses,
Rianna

Dear Rianna,

I think it's time to see your doctor about taking you off the Ritalin.

Calmly yours,
Dr. Santa

Dear Santa,

My mom and dad told me I'm spoiled and that I should think about the poor kids in Indiana because they don't have any toys and I should be thankful because I have toys and food and a nice house and they told me I should give all my presents to the poor children in Indiana but I don't think that's fair so maybe you could just bring me the toys from my list and give those kids all my old toys. Can you do that Santa?

Sin Celry
Chris Eck

Dear Chris,

While I agree that we should all feel sympathy for any child born in Indiana, I believe your mother actually said India—unless she didn't, in which case she's probably a moron. In any case, don't feel bad for the "poor" children of India. While their standard of living is still far below that of the "developed" world, they are catching up rapidly. By about the start of your second marriage (it will fail, too) India will have surpassed the United States in wealth and standard of living. You see, while all you Americans sit around complimenting yourselves about being number one, the people of India are actually educating themselves in real courses such as Microbiology and Quantum Physics—as opposed to made-up subjects like Creation Science and Hip Hop Culture. But don't worry, even as your standard of living slides inexorably toward the gutter, you'll still think you're number one—even if you don't know the difference between India and Indiana.

Thanks for caring!
Santa

Hi Santa,

My sister is making me leave out oatmeal cookies for you even though
they are gross. You probably like chocolate chip cookies better. I'll try to
put some of them on the plate too. Please don't put me on the bad list,
just my sister.

Looking out for you,
Kevyn

Dear Kevyn,

You're absolutely correct. Oatmeal cookies are disgusting. The only thing
worse are oatmeal cookies with raisins. At first glance, they look like oatmeal cookies with chocolate chips, and you think to yourself, *well, at least
these oatmeal cookies have chocolate chips.* Then you pick one up and take a
bite only to realize that they're really RAISINS! It's a joke of the cruelest
kind. Hitler LOVED oatmeal cookies with raisins!

Rest assured that you will not be punished for this travesty. Your
sister, however, shall pay.

Disgustedly yours,
Santa

Dear Santa,

Please, don't be mad but my Grandpa hit one of your reindeer with his car last night and even though he said it hurt his car more than his car hurt it I don't think it'll be good in time for Christmas Eve. My dad said you can borrow our dog Stinker if you need to because she's as big as a horse. I don't think Stinker can fly but she'll try her best.

Sorry.
Sam

Dear Sam,

Don't worry. Your grandpa didn't hit one of my reindeer. Unfortunately, he did hit a jogger—despite his claim that it was a deer. I'm afraid the police will trace the incident to him by early Christmas morning. Just as you're all opening the gifts I've left for you, they'll arrive to arrest him for manslaughter.

Enjoy the presents!
Santa

Dear Santa,

Hi! I want a puppy for Christmas. How do your elves make gifts? I hope I have been a good boy. I love my parents. Do you? Please come to my house. Do you like puppys? I hope I can see you!

You friend,
Henry Sellers

Dear Henry,

What an unusual question. Do I love my parents? To be honest, I really hadn't thought of them in years. Most people assume I'm an orphan thanks to the efforts of a publicity agency I hired back in the 1950s. They suggested going with the whole orphan thing as a way of mythologizing my past and creating an aura of mystery about my origins. The truth is that I did have parents. From an early age they trained me in the art of toy making. But did they ever let me play with the toys I created? No. They made me give them all away. Did it make me bitter? You bet. Did I take on the role of toymaker to the world in an attempt to win the favor of two nasty parents who ultimately would never be satisfied no matter how many toys I made and gave away?

Now that I finally look at it that way, I see that what I've been doing is merely an attempt to gain the love of parents whose love was never attainable in the first place. There's no point in me making and delivering all of these toys. I see that now. Finally, I'm free of this onerous task. And I owe it all to you, Henry.

Free at last,
Santa

PS: Whenever children ask me why I no longer bring them toys, I'll say it's all thanks to Henry Sellers of Evanston, Illinois.

THE COMPLEAT SHOPPER:
GEORGE PLIMPTON'S GUIDE TO GIFT GIVING

BY GEORGE PLIMPTON

Imagine that ten thousand dollars has been mysteriously set-tled into your bank account on the condition that it is to be spent on buying holiday gifts for ten of the most famous and admired citizens of the country—celebrities whose level of power and prestige is such that it truly taxes the imagination to decide what on earth to get them. A true challenge of the art of giving! This magazine gave me the opportunity a few weeks ago, along with the following list we thought would be an interesting group of beneficiaries to shop for: Woody Allen, Katharine Hepburn, Lee Iacocca, Reggie Jackson, Ted Koppel, Steve Martin, Beverly Sills, Donald Trump, Tom Wolfe, *Still Undecided*. Go to it, they said.

I should start by mentioning that I am not a good shopper—too quick to leave things to the last, confused in stores by the array of merchandise, intimidated by salespeople, inevitably hampered by lack of funds, and oversensitive to the reactions of those I have bought presents for. From my adolescent years I can still feel the pangs of guilt seeing my father unwrap a pocket comb which was all I could afford after spending my Christmas allotment for him on a movie binge. To make up for it the next year I "made" him his Christmas gift. In my family the personal touch was considered the most valued. I caught and mounted a catfish (with the help of a local taxidermist) on a board with hooks on the back so it could be hung from the wall. My father worked up as much enthusiasm as he could ("very nice, son") and it ended up on my own wall which it graced, the sawdust and so forth leaking slowly out of it, for a number of years.

Of course, the chance of seeing how the celebrities on my list would react to my gifts was nonexistent, since I do not know most of them, and have only a nodding acquaintance with the rest. On the other hand, *not* knowing Lee Iacocca, Donald Trump, *et al* meant ruling out buying the practical present, the kind that elicits the response: "How did you know? Just what I needed!" as the garden hose or the frying pan, whatever, is unveiled from its wrappings. In addition, despite the heady sensation that I had a thousand dollars available to spend on each of my celebrities, their success in life suggests that they "have everything" (certainly practical things like frying pans), which is an envious situation but one making it difficult to buy appropriate gifts.

In fact, the first notion that crossed my mind was to buy my list of people a *single* gift: a fireworks show! Why not? Fireworks are a passion of mine. Why not get it over with and spend the entire ten thousand dollar allotment on fireworks—inviting the group to a beach barbeque complete with beach blankets, insect repellents, and at nightfall giving the signal to the "pyrotechnicians" across the dunes. The show would include shells dedicated to each guest and selected to capture something of their character. I would call out through a little megaphone: "The Steve Martin!" and a madcap British-made shell named Birds and Bees would crisscross and hum helter-skelter above the sea; Beverly Sills would get a Japanese-made rose chrysanthemum; Katharine Hepburn, lolling on her beach blanket, would be saluted with the solitary silvery burst of a silver willow.

But the logistics of getting the celebrities to the beach at the same time, the thought of a heavy rainstorm or a thick fog marring the show, the problems involved in getting the elusive Katharine Hepburn to turn up, the possibility of my guests not getting along and standing by the water's edge *sulking*...all this made the concept somewhat impractical.

But something came of it. The thought of a rose chrysanthemum firework inspired the notion of what Beverly Sills, the great opera star, might like. From the Gem Antiques shop on upper Madison Avenue I bought a paperweight with roses imbedded in it. The thought behind my purchase was that a bouquet of roses, wrapped in cellophane, is inevitably rushed out from the wings after a performance; or single long-stemmed roses are tossed across the footlights by exuberant fans. But after standing in vases for a few days, paling, dropping a petal or two, the roses are thrown out. How appropriate, then, to have a permanent rose in one's house. At Gem Antiques I was told that paperweights are referred to generically, depending on what is inside: "flowerweights, creatureweights, portraitweights..." Creatureweights? I was shown a sea horse clinging to a stalk, a small snake on a bed of moss. The most valuable paperweight known is a creatureweight, 3 silkworms eating a leaf. Made circa 1860 it sold recently at auction for $143,000!

I whistled in awe and said I was looking for a flowerweight. "One with a rose. No silkworms, please!"

I picked one out by a contemporary artist called appropriately enough, Opening Night Bouquet ($649.50 including tax).

So that was Sills.

I had an idea for Steve Martin. Last spring in Atlantic City I had watched him in an abbreviated eight-minute comic sketch in which he had impersonated a magician named "The Great Flydini." Standing centerstage he unzipped his trousers, and then slowly and with great ceremony, proceeded to remove a whole series of items which he showed the audience, his eyes widening slightly as if mildly astonished at his ability to produce them, putting some of what he took out in a receptacle—an opera hat, as I recall, on a stand alongside. What emerged from his trousers included a number of eggs, a string of flags, a burst of bubbles, a lighted cigarette, a glass of wine, a puppet who sings an aria from *I Pagliacci*, and a corded telephone which rang from time to time and which Martin pulled out to answer and then put back in. Afterwards I went backstage. I asked the comedian if other objects had come to mind. He nodded and said that he often thought of "loading up" (as he put it) with a series of little men who would shoot up out of his trousers, pre-sumably propelled by rubber bands, and drift to the stage floor under brightly colored parachutes. Then he thought a little radio-controlled truck which would speed for the wings when he set it on the floor would have a "lot of audience appeal."

☠ ☠ ☠

Remembering this, and very much in agreement about "audience appeal," I paid a visit to F.A.O. Schwarz, the famous toy store on Fifth Avenue. I was introduced to a young red-haired senior buyer, Mark G. Anthony, who has been with the company for three years. I sat opposite him in his office. He seemed surprisingly blasé about my requests—as if it were quite normal to be asked to supply a platoon of parachutists and a radio-controlled vehicle capable of darting out of a magician's trousers.

"The vehicle poses us no problems," he said. "The smallest one we have is "the Chipmunk," two inches or so in length, very quick on the floor, and about the right size for Mr. Martin. That is to say it could be fitted in there very nicely, I think, when he prepares."

"He calls it 'loading up,'" I said.

"Yes. The batteries are not included with the Chipmunk," Mr. Anthony went on. "As for the parachutists, we can supply them though it may take some time and research. He'll have to figure out the catapult-ing apparatus himself." He wondered if Mr. Martin had an "engineer" who worked on such matters.

I said I assumed so.

"How many parachutists would Mr. Martin like?"

I said: "He'll lose them from time to time. They'll drift out into the audience or into the orchestra pit. I would think two dozen would get him through a year."

I left F.A.O. Schwarz with a sense of accomplishment. Since the cost of the items (approximately $84) hardly added up to Steve Martin's share I bought him handcrafted copper easels, a pair of them for $900.

He has a formidable collection of art, presumably burgeoning by the day, the wall space in his house filling up, so that a couple of easels on which to set a painting seemed practical enough.

Art also occurred to me in wondering what to buy Tom Wolfe. The title of his best-selling novel, *The Bonfire of the Vanities*, seemed so visual that perhaps I could tempt a famous artist to sketch (for $1,000) the original historic burning in 1497 in Florence of the pile of carnival masks, indecent art and so forth that was symbolic of the renunciation of worldly enjoyments...and present him with whatever was done.

I thought of Robert Rauschenberg, the distinguished contemporary artist. I was introduced to him once at a country club wedding dinner; in the uproar of the party I mistook his name for that of Bob Rosburg, the pro golfer-turned-commentator whose voice emerges from television sets during the great tournaments. Both Bobs actually resemble each other to some degree. So I doggedly kept asking Rauschenberg questions about golf (what did he think of metal drivers, and so forth), puzzled by his quick impatient gestures when I moved on to yet another golf topic. We got it straightened out, but I was nervous calling him, wondering if he'd still think I might be prodding him about, say, his putting stroke. He turned out to be in Zurich, Switzerland. I hesitatingly explained my proposal. Did anything come to mind for Tom Wolfe?

After a pause Rauschenberg said, "How about a nice quick kick in the *butt*?"

It suddenly occurred to me that Wolfe, who has written extensively on art, had slighted Rauschenberg in some way.

I winced and asked over the phone if it was an impertinence to be asking this favor. Had Wolfe written much about him?

"Not much," Rauschenberg said enigmatically. "Hey," he went on, "How about a box of ashes?"

"As long as you sign it," I said desperately.

Rauschenberg laughed and said he'd think up something. My hand was shaking slightly as I replaced the receiver in the cradle.

Well, that took care of three celebrities on my list. For possible gifts for the rest, hoping for less trauma, I thought I'd try the Hammacher Schlemmer on 57TH Street, a store which prides itself in out-of-the-ordinary presents for the kind of people who have everything. Sure enough. After a few minutes of browsing I found something I thought might work for Katharine Hepburn—a solar-powered ventilated pith helmet, ordinary-looking except for a little fan on the brim which, according to the directions, "directs a constant beam toward your forehead on a hot day." What an inspiration! Perfect for Hepburn's use in her Connecticut garden and perhaps a pleasant reminder of her association with *The African Queen*. Moreover, it turned out that Katharine Hepburn has a particular fondness for hats. When she and Henry Fonda were cast together in *On Golden Pond* she gave him a hat which had been Spencer Tracy's favorite and which *he* had received from John Ford, the director. As a reciprocal gift Fonda painted and gave Hepburn a watercolor of *his* two favorite hats, a rain hat and a fishing hat, with the Tracy-Ford hat set between them. The only problem I could think of with Hammacher Schlemmer's self-cooling helmet was that its cost ($47.95) meant that I would have to find some additional gifts for Miss Hepburn.

I continued my browsing. In the corner of the showroom I came across a small turbine-like engine described as "the Bubble Blizzard." "For use at conventions!" an accompanying sign read. Weighing six pounds, electrically powered, a fan-like apparatus on the machine could produce five hundred bubbles a minute, and it was adjustable so that the bubbles ranged from golf ball–size to "much larger!" Perhaps not the gift for Katharine Hepburn, but what about Ted Koppel? He could use the Bubble Blizzard on *Nightline*. He is the only late-night television personage who has no gimmickry on his desk. Johnny Carson has his coffee mug, of course, and a pencil to twiddle with. David letterman has *his* coffee mug, pencils he tosses over his shoulder, a telephone, and with a push of the button he can activate a minuscule fountain in front of his desk.

But Koppel? As the viewers of *Nightline* know, his desk is essentially bare. Most of the time the camera is focused on a head-and-shoulders shot of Koppel himself, or on his back as he swivels around to converse with a huge screen usually filled with the unpleasant visage of the Iranian ambassador. How appropriate to jazz this up with a Bubble Blizzard! Koppel could use it symbolically—press a button so that a large bubble, wobbling and translucent, would drift up in front of the Iranian ambassador to indicate "hot air" or whatever.

But the more I thought about the Bubble Blizzard ($199.50) for Koppel the less appealing the idea became...perhaps just the *thought* of Koppel's face—slightly arch and disdainful—as he pulled the Bubble Blizzard from its wrappings at Christmas. I would have to think of something else.

I have never had an easy time with Koppel. I once appeared on his show on July 4TH a few years ago to talk about fireworks. I was seated on the top of a sound truck in Philadelphia just after a huge display. I had a gadget in my ear so I could hear Koppel's questions. Just as we went on the air the feed—as I believe it is called—began to break up and it was extremely difficult to understand what Koppel was asking me. Straining to catch his words, I would finally blurt out, "Ted, did you just ask me if..." but by the time Koppel assured me that it was, I had half-forgotten the question.

Finally, very likely in exasperation, Koppel said as follows (as nearly as I could make out): "You have a reputation as a storyteller. Tell us a funny story about fireworks."

"Ted, did you just ask me if I could ... " etc.

I was close to a complete loss for words. There are very few "funny" stories about fireworks, at least none that quickly came to mind. After a few seconds of throat-clearing I struggled desperately through a description of a firework—indeed for a while the largest ever built—so huge that when it went off above the Saint Johns River in Florida, the concussion broke sixty-odd windows in the town of Titusville and set off dozens of burglar alarms. Hardly a "funny" story.

If my past experience was any indication, I had a feeling Koppel's was going to be the most difficult gift on my list. I moved moodily through Hammacher Schlemmer. I stared at a bright orange submersible aquarider (made by Aquascooter), a kind of torpedo powered by a two-horsepowered engine, a three-foot-long snorkel feeding air down to it, and capable of pulling a scuba diver along for three hours underwater. Not for Hepburn, or Koppel, but wouldn't *Woody Allen* like to be towed behind this apparatus? Its cost was $490, which meant that if I bought a pair, the other for Mia, Woody Allen's thousand would be spent just about to the penny. The pair could trail each other around the Caribbean, three feet down, for three hours at a time. But I remembered that Allen rarely leaves the urban world; the two aquariders would simply clutter up his entryway. So I left Hammacher Schlemmer, discouraged, with only Katharine Hepburn's pith helmet to show for my pains.

The next day, in the course of worrying about Woody Allen's gift, I came across a listing in the telephone directory: "Perfect Presents by Suzy, Ltd." I called the number to find that I was talking to Suzy herself. She explained she runs a shopping service specializing mostly in "theme" and "fun" gifts. A gift for Woody Allen? No problem! With hardly a moment's hesitation she proposed a tote bag full of items that would be useful during the course of a typical Woody Allen day. She seemed to know exactly what that would be.

"When he wakes up in the morning he'll need to interpret his dreams from the night before," she told me briskly. "So that's the first thing we'll put in his tote bag—a book on dream-interpreting. Next, a fun soap (it's shaped like a dinosaur) for his morning shower. How about two sterling silver toothpaste tube keys, engraved with Woody's and Mia's initials, for squeezing toothpaste out of the tube from the bottom?"

"Why not?"

"We have some fun toothbrushes."

"Throw them in."

"Now breakfast. We have some food packets: Irish oatmeal, scones mix, honey jars. Also a book called *Breakfast Recipes* which Woody can read while he's eating the Irish oatmeal."

She went on with hardly a pause for breath. "Now for his morning exercises so he can be in better shape for tennis."

I ventured that I was surprised Woody Allen played tennis. "He's not the first person you'd imagine on a court."

"I've *seen* him on a tennis court," Suzy assured me. "So we'll need a jump rope, an ExecuFlex stretcher, a book on stretching exercises, weights to attach to the ankles and wrists. Also, a headphone radio so he can listen to his favorite rock and roll while he exercises. Afterwards he'll have to relax...take the kinks out."

"Absolutely."

"For this I'm adding a massager and a loofah."

"A what?"

"It's a little mitt made out of natural grass for removing dry skin."

"Stick it in."

She went on through Woody Allen's afternoon and into the evening. Into the tote bag went a two-foot-long inflated dinosaur for his children along with a book on hand shadows so he could amuse them with an "eagle flying on the wall." For later in the evening she suggested four tapes from the old radio show, "The Shadow."

"He'd like that," I said, thinking of his motion picture, *Radio Days*.

"Then when it's time for bed," she went on, "we have two acrylic champagne glasses for them to toast the day, two eye masks, and two herbal pillows, and finally a little bed light so that..."

"...he can read the book on dreams?" I suggested.

"Yes," Suzy said. "And practice his hand shadows on the wall. It's a very *practical* tote bag we're putting together here!"

Suzy, who works out of a loft in New York's garment district, spent only about ten minutes on the phone "putting together" Woody Allen's tote bag (its total cost worked out as $500), and with such enthusiasm that I was tempted to turn over my entire list to her.

Instead I went back to 57th Street to the antithesis of Perfect Presents by Suzy: the Place des Antiquaires a few doors from Hammacher Schlemmer—a subterranean grid of galleries and fancy shops devoted to the "beauty and nuances of the collectors' world." An escalator bore me down to where two musicians were playing a flute and an Irish harp. Their music drifted after me. I was heading for a shop called Marine and Collections where I hoped to find a state of the art ship-in-a-bottle to give to Donald Trump, the real estate tycoon. The notion behind the gift was that Trump, despite spending $29 million buying the Khashoggi yacht, renamed the Trump Princess, does not like boats: he is not a seafaring man. What better gift, then, than a ship safely secured in a bottle, especially if I could get his name tastefully emblazoned along its side, which is what Trump tends to do with his properties. Not necessarily a utilitarian gift, but thoughtful!

On the way I passed by an antiques store, Bernard Steinitz et Fils, a famous emporium whose window-front display included an enormous bust of a Roman emperor bearing such a striking resemblance to Lee Iacocca that I wandered in to ask its price. My forlorn hope was that there is such a small market for massive busts (it must have weighed a quarter of a ton) that it might be selling for a bargain price. It was worth a try. I had to assume that Iacocca would be pleased. I have not been to his house, but presumably it has the kind of large entrance hall where such a bust might be an agreeable addition.

I was greeted by a saleswoman smartly got up in a white pantsuit. She said the bust was of Caesar—Lucius Verus Caesar, a contemporary of Marcus Aurelius about 161 A.D.

I asked how much it cost.

"$90,000."

A true budget-buster! I felt I should affect a posture of savoir-faire, which I did with a drawn-out "oh yesss," accompanied by a slight nod of agreement as if cost was not a problem, but whether the Caesar's bust was exactly what I had in mind.

"Four men can't budge it. Solid marble," she said proudly. "We have to use a hoister to move it four inches."

In quick succession I was shown a vase which could have contained the corpse of a large horse, a towering iron bird, an equestrian statue of Napolean by Jacquemart ($120,000), and had described to me a huge statue of the Sancho Panza along with his donkey.

"Sancho's out in our warehouse in New Jersey. We're trying to figure out how to get them in here."

"You've given me a lot to think about," I said.

We exchanged cards and she said she would send me a photograph of Sancho Panza. As I left I remembered that Marilyn Monroe once turned down the gift of an elephant from a maharajah on the sensible grounds that her house wasn't large enough to contain it.

Things went almost as awkwardly in Marine and Collections. The proprietor, M. Dominique Lalande, didn't have any ships-in-bottles in stock, though he told me he could order a fine example from his Paris branch. Elegant and intense, he seemed disturbed when I said I wanted some letters written on the side of the ship. He felt his craftsmen could do it by opening the bottle and reaching in with a hooked paintbrush, but it would disturb the value of the gift. "Arrache!" he said.

He seemed somewhat more understanding when I explained that the ship-in-the-bottle was for Donald Trump.

"Oh! Ah!"

He began showing me through his shop—antique French boxes, ship models of galleons under full sail, globes of the world; he suggested that what Donald Trump would truly like was a pipe which had once belonged to Ferdinand I, the Emperor of Austria. He showed it to me in its velvet-lined box—intricately carved in ivory and so massive it was difficult to imagine getting it to one's mouth without help.

"I don't think Trump smokes," I said feebly. M. Lalande snorted. "The pipe is, of course, for collectors. Next to Edmond de Rothschild I have the greatest pipe collection in the world. In fact, why do I say, 'next to?' It is equal if not *better*."

When it was evident I was going to pass up on the pipe (its cost, incidentally, a true budget-buster, was $70,000), M. Lalande announced that he was on his way to Paris the next morning. From there he would confer with me about his stock of ships-in-the-bottle. He would see to it that the one picked was properly prepared. Its approximate cost: $800.

With Trump out of the way, I still had Reggie Jackson, Lee Iacocca, and the pesky Ted Koppel to go, as well as finding something to add to Katharine Hepburn's pith helmet. I telephoned Neiman Marcus in Dallas. It, like Hammacher Schlemmer, is famous for the unique and imaginative gift—if on a somewhat grander scale. In 1962 their catalogue offered a Chinese junk "made in Hong Kong...in your choice of brightly painted or natural wood." In 1971 a "his and her" suggestion was a pair of 2000 year-old authenticated mummy cases (vacant) for $16,000; in 1980 a pair of ostriches for $1,500, and so forth. I was put through to David Wolfe, a senior vice president, who represents the Fur division. Reggie Jackson? Among his suggestions was a "fur-lined athletic supporter—all mink!" He informed me that the mink ("absolutely top-grade") could be done for about four hundred dollars.

I asked: "What about the 'comfort factor?'"

After a pause Mr. Wolfe said, "Well, a *chinchilla* would be more comfortable—in fact the *ultimate*. We could do a chinchilla for about $450."

While I was pondering this, another Neiman Marcus official, Steve Magner, a vice president of the Precious Jewels division, came on the line. He also had an idea for Reggie Jackson.

"As you know he's referred to as Mr. October for his late season brilliance. Well, the October stone is opal. Our designers can handcraft an opal into a baseball bat and mount it horizontally on a stand with the words 'Mr. October' on the base."

"Wonderful," I said truthfully.

"We can put a baseball on the base," he said.

"By all means," I said. "And the cost?"

My heart sank as he said the work would cost about $4,000. Another budget-buster! I asked what could be done for a thousand.

"The bat would be a lot smaller," Mr. Magner said.

"It's not a question of Jackson having to *squint* at it?"

"Oh, no," Mr. Magner said, "it'll be nicely discernible. The opal is a lovely stone," he went on. "It's ten percent water and reflects the colors of the rainbow. Guaranteed not to leak."

I left Mr. Magner to explain to his associate that I had picked the opal trophy over the mink (or chinchilla) athletic supporter.

Also from Neiman Marcus I ordered a clock placed in the Chrysler emblem ($500) for Lee Iacocca. I wanted to buy him a large clock set in a full-size old-fashioned gas pump I had spotted in the Norm Thompson catalogue (perfect for telling time in his garage) but, alas, it was another budget-buster—not as substantial a blow as Caesar's bust would have been, but a couple of thousand more than the Iacocca allotment. I also ordered (from the Price of His Toys catalogue) an item called a Car Revenger ($19.95), which is a radar detector-sized box for Mr. Iacocca to mount on the dashboard of his Chrysler. It has three buttons which produce "full sound and light effects"—machine gun fire and so forth—for taking out his frustration when the Chrysler is stuck in traffic jams.

To flesh out the meager amount I had spent on Katharine Hepburn's pith helmet, I ordered a "parfait" of cashmere sweaters in an oversize glass from Neiman Marcus ($827.19 including special gift wrapping with candy cane). In addition, from the Norm Thompson catalogue I sent away for a $59 set of copper wind chimes to bring "soothing sounds to her ears"—as the catalogue assured me—while in the cool of her pith helmet she worked in her Connecticut garden.

That left only Ted Koppel and the "undecided" from my original list. The ignominy of my appearance on his *Nightline* show finally suggested the perfectly appropriate gift for Koppel—a smart fireworks show! I telephoned Fireworks by Grucci in Bellport, L.I. to find out what kind of *fête du jardin* display could be arranged. For a special bargain price of $1500 Felix Grucci, Jr. offered catherine wheels, roman candles, miniature rockets and shells—a very brief show but effective. Mr. Grucci wanted me to know there was no reason why Mr. Koppel couldn't supplement the cost on his own if he *truly* wanted to dazzle his guests.

I said I would mention his suggestion in Koppel's gift notification.

That left only "undecided." After some thought I chose to forego the many candidates—among them Elizabeth Dole, Willie Mays, Nancy Reagan (whose husband on their twenty-fifth wedding anniversary gave her a canoe named TruLove), Steffi Graf, Bart Giamatti, Elizabeth Taylor (whose then-husband, Richard Burton, gave her the Krupp diamond for beating him in a ping-pong match), David Letterman, Leonard Bernstein (whose ninety-year-old mother on his seventieth birthday gave him an ancient Chinese scroll which advised him in part to listen to his mother), Tip O'Neill, Brigitte Bardot (one of whose husbands, the industrialist Gunther Sachs, displayed his love for her by dropping a planeload of red roses onto the roof of her villa), and so on. I did not think any of them would mind because I gave the thousand dollars (plus what was left after my shopping spree) to two charities: the East Harlem Tutorial, a remedial reading program for young children in that community, and Boys Harbor, which initiates any number of projects for disadvantaged kids in New York City—both associations involved in gift-giving of a kind.

My list completed, I began wondering how the gifts would be received. One of the rules in Emily Post's *Etiquette* for buying gifts is that the giver should imagine *getting* the gift. Indeed, Elsa Maxwell, the famous society personage, was known for giving presents she personally liked so much that after a few weeks, she would plead to have them returned. "I cannot *live* without my snuff box," or whatever. Knowing this, Noel Coward had a silver box he had received from her instantly engraved "To Noel from Elsa Maxwell" so that there would not be much point in her taking it back.

Though I had found a gift for everyone on my list it occurred to me I had not applied myself to the Emily Post rule, and certainly not to Elsa Maxwell's. Not many of my gifts would have delighted me had I been the recipient: certainly not the paratrooper corps springing from Steve Martin's fly; or Katharine Hepburn's pith helmet; or Iaccoca's personalized clock; or Reggie Jackson's opal bat. Donald Trump's ship-in-the-bottle would only have been a delight if depersonalized; Tom Wolfe's bonfire sketch and Beverly Sills's rose were hardly of meaning for me. Woody Allen's tote bag was tailored for his day, not mine.

Of course, Ted Koppel's fireworks show was another matter! Having received a more expensive gift than any of the others, perhaps the condition should be that Koppel would have to invite everyone on the list (including the donor) to his *fête du jardin* fireworks party. A grand evening! Everyone could compare gifts. I could ask Woody Allen if he enjoyed his herbal pillow. ☙

MERRY CHRISTMAS

BY JAMES THURBER

𝕴𝔱 didn't surprise me to learn that Americans send out a billion and a half Christmas cards every year. That would have been my guess, give or take a quarter of a billion. Missing by 250 million is coming close nowa-years, for what used to be called astronomical figures have now become the figures of earth. I am no longer staggered by the massive, but I can still be shaken by the minor human factors involved in magnificent statistics. A national budget of 71 thousand million is comprehensible to students of our warlike species, but who is to account for the rising sales of vodka in this nation—from 108,000 bottles in 1946 to 32,500,000 bottles in 1956? The complexities of federal debt and personal drinking are beyond my grasp, but I think I understand the Christmas card situation, or crisis.

It disturbed me to estimate that two-fifths of the 1956 Christmas cards, or six hundred million, were received by people the senders barely knew and could count only as the most casual of acquaintances, and that approximately thirty million recipients were persons the senders had met only once, in a bar, on a West Indies cruise, at a doctor's office, or while fighting a grass fire in Westchester. The people I get Christmas cards from every year include a Jugoslav violist I met on the *Leviathan* in 1925, the doorman of a restaurant in Soho, a West Virginia taxi driver who is writing the biography of General Beauregard, the young woman who cured my hiccoughs at Dave Chasen's in 1939 (she twisted the little finger of my left hand and made me say Garbo backward), innumerable people who know what to do about my eye and were kind enough to tell me so in hotel lobbies and between the acts of plays, seven dog owners who told me at Tim's or Bleeck's that they have a dog exactly like the one I draw, and a lovely stranger in one of these saloons who snarled at a proud dog owner: "The only dog that looks like the dog this guy draws is the dog this guy draws."

The fifteen hundred million annual Yuletide greetings are the stamp and sign of the American character. We are a genial race, as neighborly abroad as at home, fond of perpetuating the chance encounter, the golden hour, the unique experience, the prewar vacation. "I think this calls for a drink" has long been one of our national slogans. Strangers take turns ordering rounds because of a shared admiration or disdain, a suddenly discovered mutual friend in Syracuse, the same college fraternity, a similar addiction to barracuda fishing. A great and lasting friendship rarely results, but the wife of each man adds the other's name to her Christmas list. The American woman who has been married ten years or longer, at least the ones I know, sends out about two hundred Christmas cards a year, many of them to persons on the almost forgotten fringe of friendship.

I had the good luck to be present one December afternoon in the living room of a couple I know just as the mail arrived. The wife asked if we minded her glancing at the cards, but she had already read one. "My God!" she exclaimed. "The Spragues are still together! They were this really charming couple we met in Jamaica eight years ago. He had been a flier, I think, and had got banged up, and then he met Marcia—I think her name was Marcia." She glanced at the card again and said, "Yes, Marcia. Well, Philip was on leave in Bermuda and he saw her riding by in a carriage and simply knew she was the girl, although he had never laid eyes on her before in his life, so he ran out into the street and jumped up on the carriage step, and said, 'I'm going to marry you!' Would you believe it, he didn't even tell her his name, and of course he didn't know her from Adam—or Eve, I guess I ought to say—and they were married. They fell in love and got married in Bermuda. Her family was terribly opposed to it, of course, and so was his when they found out about hers, but they went right ahead anyway. It was the most romantic thing I ever heard of in my life. This was four or five years before we met them, and—"

"Why are you so astonished that they are still together?" I asked.

"Because their meeting was a kind of third-act curtain," said my friend's husband. "Boy meets girl, boy gets girl—as simple as that. All that's left is boy loses girl. Who the hell are Bert and Mandy?" he asked, studying a Christmas card.

Another greeting card category consists of those persons who send out photographs of their families every year. In the same mail that brought the greetings from Marcia and Philip, my friend found such a conversation piece. "My God, Lida is enormous!" she exclaimed. I don't know why women want to record each year, for two or three hundred people to see, the ravages wrought upon them, their mates, and their progeny by the artillery of time, but between five and seven per cent of Christmas cards, at a rough estimate, are family groups, and even the most charitable recipient studies them for little signs of dissolution or derangement. Nothing cheers a woman more, I am afraid, than the proof that another woman is letting herself go, or has lost control of her figure, or is clearly driving her husband crazy, or is obviously drinking more than is good for her, or still doesn't know what to wear. Middle-aged husbands in such photographs are often described as looking "young enough to be her son," but they don't always escape so easily, and a couple opening envelopes in the season of mercy and good will some-times handle a male friend or acquaintance rather sharply. "Good Lord!" the wife will say. "Frank looks like a sex-crazed shotgun slayer, doesn't he?" "Not to me," the husband may reply. "To me he looks more like a Wilkes-Barre dentist who is being sought by the police in connection with the disappearance of a choir singer."

Anyone who undertakes a comparative analysis of a billion and a half Christmas cards is certain to lose his way once in a while, and I now find myself up against more categories than I can handle. Somewhere in that vast tonnage of cardboard, for example, are—I am just guess-ing now—three hundred million cards from firms, companies, corpora-tions, corner stores, and other tradespeople. In the old days they sent out calendars for the New Year, and skipped Christmas, but I figure they are now responsible for about a fifth of the deluge. Still another category includes inns, bars, restaurants, institutions, councils, committees, leagues, and other organizations. One of my own 1956 cards came from the Art Department of Immaculate Heart College, in Los Angeles, whose point of contact with me has eluded my memory. A certain detective agency used to send me a laconic word every December, but last year, for some disturbing reason, I was struck off the agency's list. I don't know how I got on it in the first place, since I have never employed a private investigator to shadow anybody, but it may be that I was one of the shadowed. The agency's slogan is "When we follow him he stays followed," and its card was invariably addressed to "Mr. James Ferber." This hint of alias added a creepy note to the holidays, and, curiously enough, the sudden silence has had the same effect. A man who is disturbed when he hears from a detective agency, and when he doesn't, may be put down, I suppose, as a natural phenomenon of our nervous era.

I suddenly began wondering, in one of my onsets of panic, what becomes of all these cards. The lady in my house who adds two hundred items to the annual avalanche all by herself calmed my anxiety by telling me that most of them get burned. Later, I found out, to my dismay, that this is not actually true. There are at least nine million little girls who consider Christmas cards too beautiful to burn, and carefully preserve them. One mother told me that her garage contains fifteen large cartons filled with old Christmas cards. This, I am glad to say, is no problem of mine, but there is a major general somewhere who may have to deal with it one of these years if the accumulation becomes a national menace, hampering the movement of troops.

Ninety per cent of women employ the annual greeting as a means of fending off a more frequent correspondence. One woman admitted to me that she holds at least a dozen friends at arm's, or year's, length by turning greeting cards into a kind of annual letter. The most a man will consent to write on a Christmas card is "Hi, boy!" or "Keep pitching," but a wife often manages several hundred words. These words, in most instances, have a way of dwindling with the march of the decades, until they become highly concentrated and even cryptic, such as "Will you ever forget that ox bice cake?" or "George says to tell Jim to look out for the 36." Thus the terrible flux of December mail is made up, in considerable part, of the forgotten and the meaningless. The money spent on all these useless cryptograms would benefit some worthy cause by at least three million dollars.

The sex behind most of the billion and a half Christmas cards is, of course, the female. I should judge that about 75,000,000 cards are received annually by women from former cooks, secretaries, and hairdressers, the formerness of some of them going back as far as 1924. It is not always easy for even the most experienced woman card sender to tell an ex-hairdresser from someone she met on a night of high wind and Bacardi at Cambridge Beaches in Bermuda. The late John McNulty once solved this for my own wife by saying, "All hairdressers are named Dolores." The wonderful McNulty's gift of inspired oversimplification, like his many other gifts, is sorely missed by hundreds of us. McNulty and I, both anti-card men, never exchanged Christmas greetings, except in person or on the phone. There was a time when I drew my own Christmas cards, but I gave it up for good after 1937. In that year I had drawn what purported to be a little girl all agape and enchanted in front of a strangely ornamented Christmas tree. The cards were printed in Paris and mailed to me, two hundred of them, in Italy. We were spending Christmas in Naples. The cards were held up at the border by the Italian authorities, agents of Mussolini who suspected everything, and returned to Paris. "I should think," commented an English friend of mine, "that two hundred copies of any drawing of yours might well give the authorities pause."

One couple, to conclude this survey on an eerie note, had sent out the same engraved Christmas card every year. Last time "From John and Joan" had undergone a little change. Joan had crossed out "John and." Her friends wonder just how many of these cheery greetings the predeceased Joan has left. So passed one husband, with only a pencil stroke to mark his going. Peace on earth, good will to women. @

CHRISTMAS IS A SAD SEASON FOR THE POOR

BY JOHN CHEEVER

Christmas is a sad season. The phrase came to Charlie an instant after the alarm clock had waked him, and named for him an amorphous depression that had troubled him all the previous evening. The sky outside his window was black. He sat up in bed and pulled the light chain that hung in front of his nose. Christmas is a very sad day of the year, he thought. Of all the millions of people in New York, I am practically the only one who has to get up in the cold black of 6 a.m. on Christmas Day in the morning; I am practically the only one.

He dressed, and when he went downstairs from the top floor of the rooming house in which he lived, the only sounds he heard were the coarse sounds of sleep; the only lights burning were lights that had been forgotten. Charlie ate some breakfast in an all-night lunchwagon and took an Elevated train uptown. From Third Avenue, he walked over to Sutton Place. The neighborhood was dark. House after house put into the shine of the street lights a wall of black windows. Millions and millions were sleeping, and this general loss of consciousness generated an impression of abandonment, as if this were the fall of the city, the end of time. He opened the iron-and-glass doors of the apartment building where he had been working for six months as an elevator operator, and went through the elegant lobby to a locker room at the back. He put on a striped vest with brass buttons, a false ascot, a pair of pants with a light-blue stripe on the seam, and a coat. The night elevator man was dozing on the little bench in the car. Charlie woke him. The night elevator man told him thickly that the day doorman had been taken sick and wouldn't be in that day. With the doorman sick, Charlie wouldn't have any relief for lunch, and a lot of people would expect him to whistle for cabs.

Charlie had been on duty a few minutes when 14 rang—a Mrs. Hewing, who, he happened to know, was kind of immoral. Mrs. Hewing hadn't been to bed yet, and she got into the elevator wearing a long dress under her fur coat. She was followed by her two funny-looking dogs. He took her down and watched her go out into the dark and take her dogs to the curb. She was outside for only a few minutes. Then she came in and he took her up to 14 again. When she got off the elevator, she said, "Merry Christmas, Charlie."

"Well, it isn't much of a holiday for me, Mrs. Hewing," he said. "I think Christmas is a very sad season of the year. It isn't that people around here ain't generous—I mean I got plenty of tips—but, you see, I live alone in a furnished room and I don't have any family or anything, and Christmas isn't much of a holiday for me."

"I'm sorry, Charlie," Mrs. Hewing said. "I don't have any family myself. It is kind of sad when you're alone, isn't it?" She called her dogs and followed them into her apartment. He went down.

It was quiet then, and Charlie lighted a cigarette. The heating plant in the basement encompassed the building at that hour in a regular and profound vibration, and the sullen noises of arriving steam heat began to resound, first in the lobby and then to reverberate up through all the six-teen stories, but this was a mechanical awakening, and it didn't lighten his loneliness or his petulance. The black air outside the glass doors had begun to turn blue, but the blue light seemed to have no source; it appeared in the middle of the air. It was a tearful light, and as it picked out the empty street he wanted to cry. Then a cab drove up, and the Walsers got out, drunk and dressed in evening clothes, and he took them up to their penthouse. The Walsers got him to brooding about the dif-ference between his life in a furnished room and the lives of the people overhead. It was terrible.

Then the early churchgoers began to ring, but there were only three of these that morning. A few more went off to church at eight o'clock, but the majority of the building remained unconscious, although the smell of bacon and coffee had begun to drift into the elevator shaft.

At a little after nine, a nursemaid came down with a child. Both the nursemaid and the child had a deep tan and had just returned, he knew, from Bermuda. He had never been to Bermuda. He, Charlie, was a prisoner, confined eight hours a day to a six-by-eight elevator cage, which was confined, in turn, to a sixteen-story shaft. In one building or another, he had made his living as an elevator operator for ten years. He estimated the average trip at about an eighth of a mile, and when he thought of the thousands of miles he had travelled, when he thought that he might have driven the car through the mists above the Caribbean and set it down on some coral beach in Bermuda, he held the narrowness of his travels against his passengers, as if it were not the nature of the elevator but the pressure of their lives that confined him, as if they had clipped his wings.

He was thinking about this when the DePauls, on 9, rang. They wished him a merry Christmas.

"Well, it's nice of you to think of me," he said as they descended, "but it isn't much of a holiday for me. Christmas is a sad season when you're poor. I live alone in a furnished room. I don't have any family."

"Who do you have dinner with, Charlie?" Mrs. DePaul asked.

"I don't have any Christmas dinner," Charlie said. "I just get a sandwich."

"Oh, Charlie!" Mrs. DePaul was a stout woman with an impulsive heart, and Charlie's plaint struck at her holiday mood as if she had been caught in a cloudburst. "I do wish we could share our Christmas dinner with you, you know," she said. "I come from Vermont, you know, and when I was a child, you know, we always used to have a great many people at our table. The mailman, you know, and the schoolteacher, and just anybody who didn't have any family of their own, you know, and I wish we could share our dinner with you the way we used to, you know, and I don't see any reason why we can't. We can't have you at the table, you know, because you couldn't leave the elevator—could you?—but just as soon as Mr. DePaul has carved the goose, I'll give you a ring, and I'll arrange a tray for you, you know, and I want you to come up and at least share our Christmas dinner."

Charlie thanked them, and their generosity surprised him, but he wondered if, with the arrival of friends and relatives, they wouldn't forget their offer.

Then old Mrs. Gadshill rang, and when she wished him a merry Christmas, he hung his head.

"It isn't much of a holiday for me, Mrs. Gadshill," he said. "Christmas is a sad season if you're poor. You see, I don't have any family. I live alone in a furnished room."

"I don't have any family either, Charlie," Mrs. Gadshill said. She spoke with a pointed lack of petulance, but her grace was forced. "That is, I don't have any children with me today. I have three children and seven grandchildren, but none of them can see their way to coming East for Christmas with me. Of course, I understand their problems. I know that it's difficult to travel with children during the holidays, although I always seemed to manage it when I was their age, but people feel differently, and we mustn't condemn them for the things we can't understand. But I know how you feel, Charlie. I haven't any family either. I'm just as lonely as you."

Mrs. Gadshill's speech didn't move him. Maybe she was lonely, but she had a ten-room apartment and three servants and bucks and bucks and diamonds and diamonds, and there were plenty of poor kids in the slums who would be happy at a chance at the food her cook threw away. Then he thought about poor kids. He sat down on a chair in the lobby and thought about them.

They got the worst of it. Beginning in the fall, there was all this excitement about Christmas and how it was a day for them. After Thanksgiving, they couldn't miss it. It was fixed so they couldn't miss it. The wreaths and decorations everywhere, and bells ringing, and trees in the park, and Santa Clauses on every corner, and pictures in the magazines and newspapers and on every wall and window in the city told them that if they were good, they would get what they wanted. Even if they couldn't read, they couldn't miss it. They couldn't miss it even if they were blind. It got into the air the poor kids inhaled. Every time they took a walk, they'd see all the expensive toys in the store windows, and they'd write letters to Santa Claus, and their mothers and fathers would promise to mail them, and after the kids had gone to sleep, they'd burn the letters in the stove. And when it came Christmas morning, how could you explain it, how could you tell them that Santa Claus only visited the rich, that he didn't know about the good? How could you face them when all you had to give them was a balloon or a lollipop?

On the way home from work a few nights earlier, Charlie had seen a woman and a little girl going down Fifty-ninth Street. The little girl was crying. He guessed she was crying, he knew she was crying, because she'd seen all the things in the toy-store windows and couldn't understand why none of them were for her. Her mother did housework, he guessed, or maybe was a waitress, and he saw them going back to a room like his, with green walls and no heat, on Christmas Eve, to eat a can of soup. And he saw the little girl hang up her ragged stocking and fall asleep, and he saw the mother looking through her purse for something to put into the stocking—This reverie was interrupted by a bell on 11. He went up, and Mr. and Mrs. Fuller were waiting. When they wished him a merry Christmas, he said, "Well, it isn't much of a holiday for me, Mrs. Fuller. Christmas is a sad season when you're poor."

"Do you have any children, Charlie?" Mrs. Fuller asked.

"Four living," he said. "Two in the grave." The majesty of his lie overwhelmed him. "Mrs. Leary's a cripple," he added.

"How sad, Charlie," Mrs. Fuller said. She started out of the elevator when it reached the lobby, and then she turned. "I want to give your children some presents, Charlie," she said. "Mr. Fuller and I are going to pay a call now, but when we come back, I want to give you some things for your children."

He thanked her. Then the bell rang on 4, and he went up to get the Westons.

"It isn't much of a holiday for me," he told them when they wished him a merry Christmas. "Christmas is a sad season when you're poor. You see, I live alone in a furnished room."

"Poor Charlie," Mrs. Weston said. "I know just how you feel. During the war, when Mr. Weston was away, I was all alone at Christmas. I didn't have any Christmas dinner or a tree or anything. I just scrambled myself some eggs and sat there and cried." Mr. Weston, who had gone into the lobby, called impatiently to his wife. "I know just how you feel, Charlie," Mrs. Weston said.

💀 💀 💀

By noon, the climate in the elevator shaft had changed from bacon and coffee to poultry and game, and the house, like an enormous and complex homestead, was absorbed in the preparations for a domestic feast. The children and their nursemaids had all returned from the Park. Grandmothers and aunts were arriving in limousines. Most of the people who came through the lobby were carrying packages wrapped in colored paper, and were wearing their best furs and new clothes. Charlie continued to complain to most of the tenants when they wished him a merry Christmas, changing his story from the lonely bachelor to the poor father, and back again, as his mood changed, but this outpouring of melancholy, and the sympathy it aroused, didn't make him feel any better.

At half past one, 9 rang, and when he went up, Mr. DePaul was standing in the door of their apartment holding a cocktail shaker and a glass. "Here's a little Christmas cheer, Charlie," he said, and he poured Charlie a drink. Then a maid appeared with a tray of covered dishes, and Mrs. DePaul came out of the living room. "Merry Christmas, Charlie," she said.

"I had Mr. DePaul carve the goose early, so that you could have some, you know. I didn't want to put the dessert on the tray, because I was afraid it would melt, you know, so when we have our dessert, we'll call you."

"And what is Christmas without presents?" Mr. DePaul said, and he brought a large, flat box from the hall and laid it on top of the covered dishes.

"You people make it seem like a real Christmas to me," Charlie said. Tears started into his eyes. "Thank you, thank you."

"Merry Christmas! Merry Christmas!" they called, and they watched him carry his dinner and his present into the elevator. He took the tray and the box into the locker room when he got down. On the tray, there was a soup, some kind of creamed fish, and a serving of goose. The bell rang again, but before he answered it, he tore open the DePauls' box and saw that it held a dressing gown. Their generosity and their cocktail had begun to work on his brain, and he went jubilantly up to 12. Mrs. Gadshill's maid was standing in the door with a tray, and Mrs. Gadshill stood behind her. "Merry Christmas, Charlie!" she said. He thanked her, and tears came into his eyes again. On the way down, he drank off the glass of sherry on Mrs. Gadshill's tray. Mrs. Gadshill's contribution was a mixed grill. He ate the lamb chop with his fingers. The bell was ringing again, and he wiped his face with a paper towel and went up to 11. "Merry Christmas, Charlie," Mrs. Fuller said, and she was standing in the door with her arms full of packages wrapped in silver paper, just like a picture in an advertisement, and Mr. Fuller was beside her with an arm around her, and they both looked as if they were going to cry. "Here are some things I want you to take home to your children," Mrs. Fuller said. "And here's something for Mrs. Leary and here's something for you. And if you want to take these things out to the elevator, we'll have your dinner ready for you in a minute." He carried the things into the elevator and came back for the tray. "Merry Christmas, Charlie!" both of the Fullers called after him as he closed the door. He took their dinner and their presents into the locker room and tore open the box that was marked for him. There was an alligator wallet in it, with Mr. Fuller's initials in the corner. Their dinner was also goose, and he ate a piece of the meat with his fingers and was washing it down with a cocktail when the bell rang. He went up again. This time it was the Westons. "Merry Christmas, Charlie!" they said, and they gave him a cup of eggnog, a turkey dinner, and a present. Their gift was also a dressing gown. Then 7 rang, and when he went up, there was another dinner and some more toys. Then 14 rang, and when he went up, Mrs. Hewing was standing in the hall, in a kind of negligee, holding a pair of riding boots in one hand and some neckties in the other. She had been crying and drinking. "Merry Christmas, Charlie," she said tenderly. "I wanted to give you something, and I've been thinking about you all morning, and I've been all over the apartment, and these are the only things I could find that a man might want. These are the only things that Mr. Brewer left. I don't suppose you'd have any use for the riding boots, but wouldn't you like the neckties?" Charlie took the neckties and thanked her and hurried back to the car, for the elevator bell had rung three times.

💀 💀 💀

By three o'clock, Charlie had fourteen dinners spread on the table and the floor of the locker room, and the bell kept ringing. Just as he started to eat one, he would have to go up and get another, and he was in the middle of the Parsons' roast beef when he had to go up and get the DePauls' dessert. He kept the door of the locker room closed, for he sensed that the quality of charity is exclusive and that his friends would have been disappointed to find that they were not the only ones to try to lessen his loneliness. There were goose, turkey, chicken, pheasant, grouse, and pigeon. There were trout and salmon, creamed scallops and oysters, lobster, crab meat, whitebait, and clams. There were plum puddings, mince pies, mousses, puddles of melted ice cream, layer cakes, *Torten*, éclairs, and two slices of Bavarian cream. He had dressing gowns, neckties, cuff links, socks, and handkerchiefs, and one of the tenants had asked for his neck size and then given him three green shirts. There were a glass teapot filled, the label said, with jasmine honey, four bottles of after-shave lotion, some alabaster bookends, and a dozen steak knives. The avalanche of charity he had precipitated filled the locker room and made him hesitant, now and then, as if he had touched some wellspring in the female heart that would bury him alive in food and dressing gowns. He had made almost no headway on the food, for all the servings were preternaturally large, as if loneliness had been counted on to generate in him a brutish appetite. Nor had he opened any of the presents that had been given to him for his imaginary children, but he had drunk everything they sent down, and around him were the dregs of Martinis, Manhattans, Old-Fashioneds, champagne-and-raspberry-shrub cocktails, eggnogs, Bronxes, and Side Cars.

His face was blazing. He loved the world, and the world loved him. When he thought back over his life, it appeared to him in a rich and wonderful light, full of astonishing experiences and unusual friends. He thought that his job as an elevator operator—cruising up and down through hundreds of feet of perilous space—demanded the nerve and the intellect of a birdman. All the constraints of his life—the green walls of his room and the months of unemployment—dissolved. No one was ringing, but he got into the elevator and shot it at full speed up to the penthouse and down again, up and down, to test his wonderful mastery of space.

A bell rang on 12 while he was cruising, and he stopped in his flight long enough to pick up Mrs. Gadshill. As the car started to fall, he took his hands off the controls in a paroxysm of joy and shouted, "Strap on your safety belt, Mrs. Gadshill! We're going to make a loop-the-loop!" Mrs. Gadshill shrieked. Then, for some reason, she sat down on the floor of the elevator. Why was her face so pale, he wondered; why was she sitting on the floor? She shrieked again. He grounded the car gently, and cleverly, he thought, and opened the door. "I'm sorry if I scared you, Mrs. Gadshill," he said meekly. "I was only fooling." She shrieked again. Then she ran out into the lobby, screaming for the superintendent.

The superintendent fired Charlie and took over the elevator himself. The news that he was out of work stung Charlie for a minute. It was his first contact with human meanness that day. He sat down in the locker room and gnawed on a drumstick. His drinks were beginning to let him down, and while it had not reached him yet, he felt a miserable sober-ness in the offing. The excess of food and presents around him began to make him feel guilty and unworthy. He regretted bitterly the lie he had told about his children. He was a single man with simple needs. He had abused the goodness of the people upstairs. He was unworthy.

Then up through this drunken train of thought surged the sharp figure of his landlady and her three skinny children. He thought of them sitting in their basement room. The cheer of Christmas had passed them by. This image got him to his feet. The realization that he was in a position to give, that he could bring happiness easily to someone else, sobered him. He took a big burlap sack, which was used for col-lecting waste, and began to stuff it, first with his presents and then with the presents for his imaginary children. He worked with the haste of a man whose train is approaching the station, for he could hardly wait to see those long faces light up when he came in the door. He changed his clothes, and, fired by a wonderful and unfamiliar sense of power, he slung his bag over his shoulder like a regular Santa Claus, went out the back way, and took a taxi to the lower East Side.

The landlady and her children had just finished off a turkey, which had been sent to them by the local Democratic Club, and they were stuffed and uncomfortable when Charlie began pounding on the door, shouting "Merry Christmas!" He dragged the bag in after him and dumped the presents for the children onto the floor. There were dolls and musical toys, blocks, sewing kits, an Indian suit, and a loom, and it appeared to him that, as he had hoped, his arrival in the basement dispelled its gloom. When half the presents had been opened, he gave the landlady a bathrobe and went upstairs to look over the things he had been given for himself.

☠ ☠ ☠

Now, the landlady's children had already received so many presents by the time Charlie arrived that they were confused with receiving, and it was only the landlady's intuitive grasp of the nature of charity that made her allow the children to open some of the presents while Charlie was still in the room, but as soon as he had gone, she stood between the children and the presents that were still unopened. "Now, you kids have had enough already," she said. "You kids have got your share. Just look at the things you got there. Why, you ain't even played with the half of them. Mary Anne, you ain't even looked at that doll the Fire Department give you. Now, a nice thing to do would be to take all this stuff that's left over to those poor people on Hudson Street—them Deckkers. They ain't got nothing." A beatific light came into her face when she realized that she could give, that she could bring cheer, that she could put a healing finger on a case needier than hers, and—like Mrs. DePaul and Mrs. Weston, like Charlie himself and like Mrs. Deckker, when Mrs. Deckker was to think, subsequently, of the poor Shannons—first love, then charity, and then a sense of power drove her. "Now, you kids help me get all this stuff together. Hurry, hurry, hurry," she said, for it was dark then, and she knew that we are bound, one to another, in licentious benevolence for only a single day, and that day was nearly over. She was tired, but she couldn't rest, she couldn't rest. ☠

CHRISTMAS DREAMS AND CRUEL MEMORIES

BY HUNTER S. THOMPSON

That's about it for now, Jann. This story is too depressing to have to confront professionally in these morbid weeks before Christmas ... I have only vague memories of what it's like there in New York, but sometimes I have flashbacks about how it was to glide in perfect speedy silence around the ice rink in front of NBC while junkies and federal informants in white beards and sleazy red jumpsuits worked the crowd mercilessly for nickels and dollars and dimes covered with Crack residue.

I remember one Christmas morning in Manhattan when we got into the Empire State Building and went up to the Executive Suite of some famous underwear company and shoved a 600-pound red tufted-leather Imperial English couch out of a corner window on something like the eighty-fifth floor ...

The wind caught it, as I recall, and it sort of drifted around the corner onto Thirty-fourth Street, picking up speed on its way down, and hit the striped awning of a Korean market, you know, the kind that sells everything from kimchi to Christmas trees. The impact blasted watermelons and oranges and tomatoes all over the sidewalk. We could barely see the impact from where we were, but I remember a lot of activity on the street when we came out of the elevator ... It looked like a war zone. A few gawkers were standing around in a blizzard, muttering to each other and looking dazed. They thought it was an underground explosion— maybe a subway or a gas main.

Just as we arrived on the scene, a speeding cab skidded on some watermelons and slammed into a Fifth Avenue bus and burst into flames. There was a lot of screaming and wailing of police sirens. Two cops began fighting with a gang of looters who had emerged like ghosts out of the snow and were running off with hams and turkeys and big jars of caviar ... Nobody seemed to think it was strange. *What the hell? Shit happens. Welcome to the Big Apple. Keep alert. Never ride in open cars or walk too close to a tall building when it snows* ... There were Christmas trees scattered all over the street and cars were stopping to grab them and speeding away. We stole one and took it to Missy's place on the Bowery, because we knew she didn't have one. But she wasn't home, so we put the tree out on the fire escape and set it on fire with kerosene.

💀 💀 💀

That's how I remember Xmas in New York, Jann. It was always a time of angst and failure and turmoil. Nobody ever seemed to have any money on Christmas. Even rich people were broke and jabbering frantically on their telephones about Santa Claus and suicide or joining a church with no rules ... The snow was clean and pretty for the first twenty or thirty minutes around dawn, but after that it was churned into filthy mush by drunken cabbies and garbage compactors and shitting dogs.

Anybody who acted happy on Christmas was lying—even the ones who were getting paid $500 an hour ... The Jews were especially sulky, and who could blame them? The birthday of Baby Jesus is always a nervous time for people who know that ninety days later they will be accused of murdering him.

So what? We have our *own* problems, eh? Jesus! I don't know how you can ride all those motorcycles around in the snow, Jann. Shit, we can *all* handle the back wheel coming loose in a skid. But the *front* wheel is something else—and that's what happens when it snows. WHACKO. One minute you feel as light and safe as a snowflake, and the next minute you're sliding sideways under the wheels of a Bekins van ... Nasty traffic jams, horns honking, white limos full of naked Jesus freaks going up on the sidewalk in low gear to get around you and the mess you made on the street ... *Goddamn this scum. They are more and more in the way. And why aren't they home with their families on Xmas? Why do they need to come out here and die on the street like iron hamburgers?*

I hate these bastards, Jann. And I suspect you feel the same ... They might call us bigots, but at least we are *Universal* bigots. Right? Shit on those people. Everybody you see these days might have the power to get you locked up ... Who knows why? They will have reasons straight out of some horrible Kafka story, but in the end it won't matter any more than a full moon behind clouds. Fuck them.

Christmas hasn't changed much in twenty-two years, Jann—not even 2000 miles west and 8000 feet up in the Rockies. It is still a day that only amateurs can love. It is all well and good for children and acid freaks to believe in Santa Claus—but it is still a profoundly morbid day for us working professionals. It is unsettling to know that one out of every twenty people you meet on Xmas will be dead this time next year ... Some people can accept this, and some can't. That is why God made whiskey, and also why Wild Turkey comes in $300 shaped canisters during most of the Christmas season, and also why criminal shitheads all over New York City will hit you up for $100 tips or they'll twist your windshield wipers into spaghetti and urinate on your door handles.

💀 💀 💀

People all around me are going to pieces, Jann. My whole support system has crumbled like wet sugar cubes. That is why I try never to employ anyone over the age of twenty. Every Xmas after that is like another notch down on the ratchet, or maybe a few more teeth off the flywheel ... I remember on Xmas in New York when I was trying to sell a Mark VII Jaguar with so many teeth off the flywheel that the whole drivetrain would lock up and whine every time I tried to start the engine for a buyer ... I had to hire gangs of street children to muscle the car back and forth until the throw-out gear on the starter was lined up very precisely to engage the few remaining teeth on the flywheel. On some days I would leave the car idling in a fireplug zone for three or four hours at a time and pay the greedy little bastards a dollar an hour to keep it running and wet-shined with fireplug water until a buyer came along.

We got to know each other pretty well after nine or ten weeks, and they were finally able to unload it on a rich artist who drove as far as the toll plaza at the far end of the George Washington Bridge, where the engine seized up and exploded like a steam bomb. "They had to tow it away with a firetruck," he said. "Even the leather seats were on fire. They laughed at me."

💀 💀 💀

And that's about it for now, Jann. Christmas is on us and it's all downhill from here on . . . At least until Groundhog Day, which is soon . . . So, until then, at least, take my advice as your family doctor, and don't do *anything* that might cause either one of us to have to appear before the Supreme Court of the United States. If you know what I'm saying . . . 💀

AGAINST WINTER

BY CHARLES SIMIC

The truth is dark under your eyelids.
What are you going to do about it?
The birds are silent; there's no one to ask.
All day long you'll squint at the gray sky.
When the wind blows you'll shiver like straw.

A meek little lamb you grew your wool
Till they came after you with huge shears.
Flies hovered over your open mouth,
Then they, too, flew off like the leaves,
The bare branches reached after them in vain.

Winter coming. Like the last heroic soldier
Of a defeated army, you'll stay at your post,
Head bared to the first snowflake.
Till a neighbor comes to yell at you,
You're crazier than the weather, Charlie.

CHRISTMAS FREUD

BY DAVID RAKOFF

J am the Ghost of Christmas Subconscious. I am the anti-Santa. I am Christmas Freud. People tell me what they wish for. I tell them the ways their wishes are unhealthy, or wished for in error.

My impersonation merely involves me sitting in a chair, either writing or reading the *Times* or *The Interpretation of Dreams* every Saturday and Sunday from late November until Christmas. I sit in a mock study facing Madison Avenue at Sixty-first Street. My study has the requisite chair and couch. It is also equipped with a motorized track on which a video camera–wielding baby carriage travels back and forth, a slide projector, a large revolving black-and-white spiral, two hanging torsos, and about ten video monitors that play Freud-related text and images: trains entering tunnels, archetypal mothers, title cards that read "I DREAMED," etc.

When I sit down in the chair for the first time, I am horrified at the humiliation of this and I have no idea how I'm going to get through four weekends of sitting here on display. This role raises unprecedented performance questions for me. For starters, should I act as though I had no idea there were people outside my window? I opt for covering my embarrassment with a kind of Olympian humorlessness. If they want twinkles, that's Santa's department.

I am gnawed at by two fears: one, that I'm being upstaged by Linda Evans's wig in the "Blondes of the Twentieth Century" window next door, and two, that a car—a taxi most likely—will suddenly lose control, come barreling through my window, and kill me. An ignoble end, to be sure. A life given in the service of retail.

Sometimes, for no clear reason, entire crowds make the collective decision not to breach a respectful six-foot distance from the window. Other times, they crowd in, attempting to read what I'm writing over my shoulder. I thank god for my illegible scrawl.

Easily half the people do not have any idea who I'm supposed to be. They wave, as if Freud were Garfield. Others snap photos. The waves are the kind of tiny juvenile hand crunches one gives to something either impossibly young and tiny or adorably fluffy. *"Oh, look it's Freud. Isn't he just the cutest thing you ever saw? Awww, I just want to bundle him up and take him home!"*

There are also the folks who are more concerned with whether or not I'm real—this I find particularly laughable since where on earth would they make mannequins that look so Jewish?

My friend David came up yesterday and was writing down what people were saying outside:

> *"Hey, he really looks like him, only younger."*
> *"Wait a sec. That's a real guy."*
> *"He just turned the page. Is he allowed to do that?"*
> *"Who is that, Professor Higgins?"*

If psychoanalysis was late nineteenth-century secular Judaism's way of constructing spiritual meaning in a post-religious world, and retail is the late twentieth century's way of constructing meaning in a post-religious world, what does it mean that I'm impersonating the father of psychoanalysis in a store window to commemorate a religious holiday?

☠ ☠ ☠

In the window, I fantasize about starting an entire Christmas Freud movement. Christmas Freuden everywhere, providing grown-ups and children alike with the greatest gift of all: insight. In department stores across America, people leave display window couches, snifflingly and meaningfully whispering, "Thank you, Christmas Freud," shaking his hand fervently, their holiday angst, if not dispelled, at least brought into starker relief. Christmas Freud on the cover of *Cigar Aficionado* magazine; Christmas Freud appearing on *Friends*; people grumbling that, here it is not even Thanksgiving and already stores are running ads with Christmas Freud's visage asking the question, *"What do women want ... for Christmas?"*

If it caught on, all the stores would have to compete. Bergdorf Goodman would leap into action with a C.G. Jung window—a near-perfect stimulation of a bear cave, while the Melanie Klein window at Niketown would have them lined up six deep, and neighborhood groups would object to the saliva and constant bell-ringing in Baby Gap's B.F. Skinner window.

@ @ @

There is an unspeakably handsome man outside the window right now, writing something down. I hope it is his phone number. How do I indicate to the woman in the fur coat, in benevolent Christmas Freud fashion, of course, to get the hell out of the way? Then again, how does one cruise someone through a department store window? Should I press my own number up against the glass? Like some polar bear in the zoo holding up a sign reading, *"Help, I'm being held prisoner!"* I feel like a birthday clown at a party for potentially violent grown-ups.

One day, I come up to the store for a photo-op for a news story about the holiday windows of New York. It is my second birthday. I am paired with a little girl named Sasha. By strange coincidence, it's her birthday, as well. She is turning ten. She is strikingly beautiful and appears in the Howard Stern movie. She is to be my patient for the photographers; it's all somewhat Alice Liddell and Charles Dodgson.

In true psychoanalytic fashion, I make her lie down and face away from me. I explain to her a little about Freud, and we play a word association game. I say *"center,"* she responds, *"of attention."* I ask her her dreams and aspirations for this, the coming eleventh year of her life. *"To make another feature and to have my role on* One Life to Live *continue."* She sells every word she says to me, smiling with both sets of teeth, her gem-like eyes glittering. She might as well be saying *"Crunchy!"* the entire time. But she is charming. I experience extreme countertransference.

I read a bit from *The Interpretation of Dreams* to her.

"Is this boring?" I ask.

"Oh no, it's relaxing. I've been working since five o'clock this morning. Keep going."

Even though her eyes are closed, she senses the light from the news cameras on her. She curls toward it like a plant and clutches her dolly in a startlingly un-childlike manner. The glass of the window fairly fogs up.

@ @ @

I've decided to start seeing patients. I'm simply not man enough to sit exposed in a window doing nothing; it's too humiliating and too boring. My patients are all people I know. Perhaps it is because the window faces away from both the street and myself that the sessions are strangely intimate and genuine. But it's more than that. The window is, surprisingly enough, very cozy. More like a children's hideaway than a fishbowl. Patients seem to relax immediately upon lying down.

S. begins the session laughing at the artifice, and ends it crying on the sofa talking about an extramarital affair. Christmas Freud is prepared and hands her a handkerchief.

K. has near-crippling tendonitis and wears huge padded orthopedic boots. The people watching think it's a fashion statement. She wears a dress from Loehmann's, but I treat her anyway.

H., a journalist, likes to talk with children, and write about them. Perhaps that is why his shirt is irregularly buttoned.

B. is a woman who only entered counseling once, briefly, to decide which of the two men she was seeing she would choose. When she made her selection, she terminated therapy. I have distaste for her glacial pragmatism. I am also amazed, as a day when I am no longer in therapy seems as distant and fictive as a future of jet packs and Smell-o-Vision.

I. is not happy in his relationship. His boyfriend stands outside the window in the gray drizzle for the entire session, his face a mask of dejection. He knows exactly what we are talking about, although he cannot hear a thing we're saying.

In fact, the real transgression, in this age of tell-all television, is not that therapy, no matter how sham, is being conducted in a store window. It is that its particulars remain private and confidential.

I'm told that a woman outside the window wondered aloud if I was an actual therapist. I suppose there must be one in this town who would jeopardize his or her credibility in that way. *"I've scheduled our next session for the window at Barney's, I hope that's OK...huh...you seem really resistant. Do you want to talk about it?"*

A journalist is doing a story on the windows for the *Times*. He asks me if this is a dream come true. *"Well, it is a dream. It's logical,"* I reply. *"One of my parents is a psychiatrist and the other is a department store window."* He doesn't laugh at my joke, but it's half true. One of my parents *is* a psychiatrist, and the other is an M.D. who also does psychotherapy. I've been in therapy myself for many, many years. The difference between seeing a shrink and being a shrink is not only less pronounced than I imagined it might be, it feels intoxicating. When my own therapist says to me, *"I have a fantasy of coming by the window and being treated by you,"* I think, *Of course you do*. I feel finally and blissfully triumphant.

My father tells me a dream he had in which I have essentially analyzed and exposed him. It's the only indication I've gotten from him so far that he is anything other than amused at what is basically a mockery of what he does. In a certain sense, I'm not just aping my father and my mother, but their father, in a way—the man who spawned their profession. And when I sit there with a patient on my couch, a pipe in my mouth, listening, it feels so ... perfect. Like any psychiatrist's kid, I know enough from growing up, and from my own years on the couch, to not ask open-ended questions, to let the silences play themselves out or not, to say gently, *"Our time is up,"* after forty-five minutes. The charade feels real, the conclusion of an equation years in the making. And more than that; it is different from being in a play. The words I speak are my own.

Even the media coverage for this escapade is extensive and strange. People from newspapers and television are asking me these deep questions about the holiday, the nature of alienation at this time of year, the subtextual meaning of gifts, things like that, as though I actually *was* Freud. It's disconcerting because with very little effort, I could be drunk with the power. But it also points out the O. Henry *Gift of the Magi* quality of it all. The media is so desperate for any departure from the usual holiday drivel they have to churn out, they come flocking. And yet, the public doesn't particularly want to read about the holiday in the first place. It's like trying to jazz up a meal nobody wanted to eat anyway.

💀 💀 💀

I get a call from the store that Allen Ginsberg might be in the Beats window on Sunday and, if he wants to, would I speak with him. *"I have no sway over Mr. Ginsberg, but if he has something he'd really like to talk about, I'm certainly available,"* I reply. Not entirely true—I'm pretty well booked.

The whole Allen Ginsberg thing depresses me a bit. Then again, if he can see it as some cosmic joke, why can't I? I feel indignant and very territorial. *Imposters only! No real ones in the window!* Anyway, it's moot, he doesn't show.

💀 💀 💀

There is a street fair outside that seems to have brought a decidedly scarier type of spectator. They are like a crowd at a carnival sideshow and I'm the Dog-faced Boy. A grown woman sticks her tongue out at me. Later, during a session, a man in his fifties presses his nose up against the window, getting grease on the glass, presses his ear up to hear and screams inaudible things at me. Today may be the day some group of thick-necks say, *"Man, that Freud guy's a fag. Let's beat the crap out of him!"*

💀 💀 💀

When I leave after each stint, I put up a little glass sign that reads, "Freud will be back soon." It's like a warning. The post-modern version of "Christ is coming. Repent!" "Freud will be back soon, whether you like it or not." "Freud will be back soon, stop deceiving yourselves." In the affluent downtown neighborhood in Toronto in which I was raised, someone had spray painted on a wall, "Mao lives!" to which someone else had added, "Here?"

💀 💀 💀

My window is a haven in midtown. I can sit here, unmindful of the crush in the aisles of the store, the hour badly spent over gifts thoughtlessly and desperately bought. As I sit here, I hear the songs that play for the blondes display, one window over. Doris Day singing "My Secret Love," Mae West singing "My Old Flame," Marlene Dietrich's rendition of "Falling in Love Again." As I listen, I feel that they're really referring to *my* window, to Freud. Every time they come up on the repeating tape loop, I find them almost unutterably poignant, with all their talk of clandestine love, erotic fixation, and painfully hidden romantic agenda. But, they might also just as easily be referring to this time of year, with the aching sadness and loneliness that seems to imbue everything. Where is that perfect object, that old flame, that secret love that eludes us? Unfindable. Unpurchasable.

💀 💀 💀

This is my final weekend as Christmas Freud, and I am starting to feel bereft in anticipation of having to take down my shingle. I started off as a monkey on display, and have wound up uncomfortably caught between joking and deadly serious. A persona that seems laughable at times, fated for me at others. I know this will fade, but for now, I want nothing more than to continue to sit in my chair, someone on the couch, and to ask them, with real concern, *"So tell me. How is everything?"*

WOMEN

BY CHARLES BUKOWSKI

I saw Sara every three or four days, at her place or at mine. We slept together but there was no sex. We came close but we never quite got to it. Drayer Baba's precepts held strong.

We decided to spend the holidays together at my place, Christmas and New Year's.

Sara arrived about noon on the 24th in her Volks van. I watched her park, then went out to meet her. She had lumber tied to the roof of the van. It was to be my Christmas present: she was going to build me a bed. My bed was a mockery: a simple box spring with the innards sticking out of the mattress. Sara had also brought an organic turkey plus the trimmings. I was to pay for that and the white wine. And there were some small gifts for each of us.

We carried in the lumber and the turkey and the sundry bits and pieces. I placed the box spring, mattress and headboard outside and put a sign on them: "Free." The headboard went first, the box spring second, and finally somebody took the mattress. It was a poor neighborhood.

I had seen Sara's bed at her place, slept in it, and had liked it. I had always disliked the average mattress, at least the ones I was able to buy. I had spent over half my life in beds which were better suited for somebody shaped like an angleworm.

Sara had built her own bed, and she was to build me another like it. A solid wood platform supported by 7 four-by-four legs (the seventh directly in the middle) topped by a layer of firm 4-inch foam. Sara had some good ideas. I held the boards and Sara drove home the nails. She was good with a hammer. She only weighed 105 pounds but she could drive a nail. It was going to be a fine bed.

It didn't take Sara long.

Then we tested it—non-sexually—as Drayer Baba smiled over us.

@@@ @@@ @@@

We drove around looking for a Christmas tree. I wasn't too anxious to get a tree (Christmas had always been an unhappy time in my childhood) and when we found all the lots empty, the lack of a tree didn't bother me. Sara was unhappy as we drove back. But after we got in and had a few glasses of white wine she regained her spirits and went about hanging Christmas ornaments, lights, and tinsel everywhere, some of the tinsel in my hair.

I had read that more people committed suicide on Christmas Eve and on Christmas Day than at any other time. The holiday had little or nothing to do with the Birth of Christ, apparently.

All the radio music was sickening and the t.v. was worse, so we turned it off and she phoned her mother in Maine. I spoke to Mama too and Mama was not all that bad.

"At first," said Sara, "I was thinking about fixing you up with Mama but she's older than you are."

"Forget it."

"She had nice legs."

"Forget it."

"Are you prejudiced against old age?"

"Yes, everybody's old age but mine."

"You act like a movie star. Have you always had women 20 or 30 years younger than you?"

"Not when I was in my twenties."

"All right then. Have you ever had a woman older than you, I mean lived with her?"

"Yeah, when I was 25 I lived with a woman 35."

"How'd it go?"

"It was terrible. I fell in love."

"What was terrible?"

"She made me go to college."

"And that's terrible?"

"It wasn't the kind of college you're thinking of. She was the faculty, and I was the student body."

"What happened to her?"

"I buried her."

"With honors? Did you kill her?"

"Booze killed her."

"Merry Christmas."

"Sure. Tell me about yours."

"I pass."

"Too many?"

"Too many, yet too few."

💀 💀 💀

Sara was preparing the turkey dressing and I sat in the kitchen talking to her. We were both sipping white wine.

The phone rang. I went and got it. It was Debra. "I just wanted to wish you a Merry Christmas, wet noodle."

"Thank you, Debra. And a happy Santa Claus to you."

We talked a while, then I went back and sat down.

"Who was that?"

"Debra."

"How is she?"

"All right, I guess."

"What did she want?"

"She sent Christmas greetings."

"You'll like this organic turkey, and the stuffing is good too. People eat poison, pure poison. America is one of the few countries where cancer of the colon is prevalent."

"Yeah, my ass itches a lot, but it's just my hemorrhoids. I had them cut out once. Before they operate they run this snake up your intestine with a little light attached and they peek into you looking for cancer. That snake is pretty long. They just run it up you!"

The phone rang again. I went and got it. It was Cassie. "How are you doing?"

"Sara and I are preparing a turkey."

"I miss you."

"Merry Christmas to you too. How's the job going?"

"All right. I'm off until January 2nd."

"Happy New Year, Cassie!"

"What the hell's the matter with you?"

"I'm a little airy. I'm not used to white wine so early in the day."

"Give me a call some time."

"Sure."

I walked back into the kitchen. "It was Cassie. People phone on Christmas. Maybe Drayer Baba will call."

"He won't."

"Why?"

"He never spoke aloud. He never spoke and he never touched money."

"That's pretty good. Let me eat some of that raw dressing."

"O.K."

"Say—not bad!"

Then the phone rang again. It worked like that. Once it started ringing it kept ringing. I walked into the bedroom and answered it.

"Hello," I said. "Who's this?"

"You son-of-a-bitch. Don't you know?"

"No, not really." It was a drunken female.

"Guess."

"Wait. I know! It's *Iris!*"

"Yes, *Iris*. And I'm pregnant!"

"Do you know who the father is?"

"What difference does it make?"

"I guess you're right. How are things in Vancouver?"

"All right. Goodbye."

"Goodbye."

I walked back into the kitchen again.

"It was the Canadian belly dancer," I told Sara.

"How's she doing?"

"She's just full of Christmas cheer."

Sara put the turkey in the oven and we went into the front room. We talked small talk for some time. Then the phone rang again. "Hello," I said.

"Are you Henry Chinaski?" It was a young male voice.

"Yes."

"Are you Henry Chinaski, the writer?"

"Yeah."

"Really?"

"Yeah."

"Well, we're a gang of guys from Bel Air and we really dig your stuff, man! We dig it so much that we're going to *reward* you, man!"

"Oh?"

"Yeah, we're coming over with some 6-packs of beer."

"Stick that beer up your ass."

"What?"

"I said, 'Stick it up your ass!'"

I hung up.

"Who was that?" asked Sara.

"I just lost 3 or 4 readers from Bel Air. But it was worth it."

The turkey was done and I pulled it out of the oven, put it on a platter, moved the typer and all my papers off the kitchen table, and placed the turkey there. I began carving as Sara came in with the vegetables. We sat down. I filled my plate, Sara filled hers. It looked good.

"I hope that one with the tits doesn't come by again," said Sara. She looked very upset at the thought.

"If she does I'll give her a piece."

"*What?*"

I pointed to the turkey. "I said, 'I'll give her a piece.' You can watch."

Sara screamed. She stood up. She was trembling. Then she ran into the bedroom. I looked at my turkey. I couldn't eat it. I had pushed the wrong button again. I walked into the front room with my drink and sat down. I waited 15 minutes and then I put the turkey and the vegetables in the refrigerator.

💀 💀 💀

Sara went back to her place the next day and I had a cold turkey sandwich about 3PM. About 5PM there was a terrific pounding on the door. I opened it up. It was Tammie and Arlene. They were cruising on speed. They walked in and jumped around, both of them talking at once.

"Got anything to *drink?*"

"Shit, Hank, ya got *anything* to drink?"

"How was your *fucking* Christmas?"

"Yeah. How was your fucking *Christmas*, man?"

"There's some beer and wine in the icebox," I told them.

(You can always tell an old-timer: he calls a refrigerator an icebox.)

They danced into the kitchen and opened the icebox.

"Hey, here's a *turkey!*"

"We're hungry, Hank! Can we have some turkey?"

"Sure."

Tammie came out with a leg and bit into it. "Hey, this is an awful turkey! It needs spices!"

Arlene came out with slices of meat in her hands. "Yeah, this needs spices. It's too mellow! You got any spices?"

"In the cupboard," I said.

They jumped back into the kitchen and began sprinkling on the spices.

"There! That's better!"

"Yeah, it *tastes* like something now!"

"Organic turkey, shit!"

"Yeah, it's shit!"

"I want some *more!*"

"Me too. But it needs *spices.*"

Tammie came out and sat down. She had just about finished the leg. Then she took the leg bone, bit and broke it in half, and started chewing the bone. I was astonished. She was eating the leg bone, spitting splinters out on the rug.

"Hey, you're eating the bone!"

"Yeah, it's *good!*"

Tammie ran back into the kitchen for some more.

Soon they both came out, each of them with a bottle of beer.

"Thanks, Hank."

"Yeah, thanks, man."

They sat there sucking at the beers.

"Well," said Tammie, "we gotta get going."

"Yeah, we're going out to rape some junior high school boys!"

"Yeah!"

They both jumped up and they were gone out the door. I walked into the kitchen and looked into the refrig. That turkey looked like it had been mauled by a tiger—the carcass had simply been ripped apart. It looked obscene.

Sara drove over the next evening.

"How's the turkey?" she asked.

"O.K."

She walked in and opened the refrigerator door. She screamed. Then she ran out.

"My god, what *happened?*"

"Tammie and Arlene came by. I don't think they had eaten for a week."

"Oh, it's sickening. It hurts my heart!"

"I'm sorry. I should have stopped them. They were on uppers."

"Well, there's just one thing I can do."

"What's that?"

"I can make you a nice turkey soup. I'll go get some vegetables."

"All right." I gave her a twenty.

Sara prepared the soup that night. It was delicious. When she left in the morning she gave me instructions on how to heat it up.

☠ ☠ ☠

Tammie knocked on the door around 4PM. I let her in and she walked straight to the kitchen. The refrigerator door opened.

"Hey, soup, huh?"

"Yeah."

"Is it any good?"

"Yeah."

"Mind if I try some?"

"O.K."

I heard her put it on the stove. Then I heard her dipping in there.

"God! This stuff is *mild!* It needs *spices!*"

I heard her spooning the spices in. Then she tried it.

"That's *better!* But it needs more! I'm *Italian,* you know. Now . . . there . . . that's better! Now I'll let it heat up. Can I have a beer?"

"All right."

She came in with her bottle and sat down.

"Do you miss me?" she asked.

"You'll never know."

"I think I'm going to get my job back at the Play Pen."

"Great."

"Some good tippers come in that place. One guy he tipped me 5 bucks each night. He was in love with me. But he never asked me out. He just ogled me. He was strange. He was a rectal surgeon and sometimes he masturbated as he watched me walking around. I could smell the stuff on him, you know."

"Well, you got him off..."

"I think the soup is ready. Want some?"

"No thanks."

Tammie went in and I heard her spooning it out of the pot. She was in there a long time. Then she came out.

"Could you lend me a five until Friday?"

"No."

"Then lend me a couple of bucks."

"No."

"Just give me a dollar then."

I gave Tammie a pocketful of change. It came to a dollar and thirty-seven cents.

"Thanks," she said.

"It's all right."

Then she was gone out of the door.

☠ ☠ ☠

Sara came by the next evening. She seldom came by this often, it was something about the holiday season, everybody was lost, half-crazy, afraid. I had the white wine ready and poured us both a drink.

"How's the Inn going?" I asked her.

"Business is crappy. It hardly pays to stay open."

"Where are your customers?"

"They've all left town; they've all gone somewhere."

"All our schemes have holes in them."

"Not all of them. Some people just keep making it and making it."

"True."

"How's the soup?"

"Just about finished."

"Did you like it?"

"I didn't have too much."

Sara walked into the kitchen and opened the refrigerator door.

"What happened to the soup? It looks strange."

I heard her tasting it. Then she ran to the sink and spit it out.

"Jesus, it's been poisoned! What happened? Did Tammie and Arlene come back and eat *soup* too?"

"Just Tammie."

Sara didn't scream. She just poured the remainder of the soup into the sink and ran the garbage disposal. I could hear her sobbing, trying not to make any sound. That poor organic turkey had had a rough Christmas. 💀

THE TRUTH ABOUT SANTA
(AN APOCALYPTIC HOLIDAY TALE)

BY GREG KOTIS

The play takes place between Christmas Eve and Christmas morning in a number of locations including:

Santa's workshop
A cozy living room
Santa's compound
A church
Ice fields somewhere near the North Pole

The cast of characters, in order of appearance, are:

JO-JO .... A kindly elf, easily spooked.
JIM-JIM .... A hard-case elf, nobody's fool.
GEORGE .... 30s/40s, a jealous man, off the wagon.
MARY .... 30s/40s, resourceful, ready for a change.
FREYA .... 10 or so, their daughter.
LUKE .... 7 or so, their son.
SANTA .... Spirit of Christmas.
MRS. CLAUS .... Santa's wife.

SCENE 2

(A cozy living room, late at night. A Christmas tree sits in the corner, aglow with lights and ornaments. The front door bursts open and George stumbles in, a bottle in each hand, sloppy drunk. He drinks heavily, then, noticing the Christmas tree, throws a bottle noisily to the ground.)

GEORGE

(Meanly, to himself)

What the Hell is this?

(From offstage we hear Mary.)

MARY(O.S.)

George?

GEORGE

She's got it all…got it all tarted up. Like a tart in a tart-house. Not in my house, pretty lady. Not tonight.

(George drinks heavily. Mary enters. She wears slippers and a robe.)

MARY

George?

(Seeing George)

Oh. Oh, no.

GEORGE

What'd I tell you about that tree?

MARY

George, please, the children. You'll wake them.

GEORGE

I'll wake them?! Yeah, I'll wake them!

(From offstage we hear Freya.)

FREYA(O.S.)

Mama?!

MARY

Go to bed, sweetie!

FREYA(O.S.)

Is that Santa?! Is he here?!

LUKE(O.S.)

Santa's here?!

MARY

Not yet, children! Now go to sleep, or he won't come!

GEORGE

No, he won't come!

MARY

What did you do to yourself?

GEORGE

What did I do?! What did YOU do—to that TREE?!

MARY

It's a Christmas tree!

GEORGE

CHRISTMAS?! You take those bangles off of her.

MARY

George—

GEORGE

I said you take those chick-a-chacks offa that tree!

MARY

They're ornaments!

GEORGE

What do you think she is, a street-walker?! She's a tree, pretty lady! Trees are pure. Least they used to be.

MARY

You promised you wouldn't do this.

GEORGE

Oh, yeah?! And what about MARRIAGE vows?! Those are promises, aren't they?! A kind of promise!

MARY

I have no idea what you're talking about!

GEORGE

And what did you do to those boxes?! Fancy pants?! Is that what you got them in?!

MARY

I wrapped them, George. They're presents.

GEORGE

They're fancy pants! I'm taking them off!

(Mary pulls a sauce pan out from under her robe. She brandishes the pan threateningly.)

MARY

Oh no, you won't.

GEORGE

(Scornfully)

What's that suppose to be? A pan?

MARY

I don't want to hurt you.

GEORGE

Didn't stop you from breaking all the marriage vows in the world, now did it?! Didn't stop you from fancy pants! So you take those bangles off-a her! You strip those pants, or so help me—YEAH, OKAY!!

(George charges the tree. Mary winds up and smacks George soundly across the face with a satisfying "pang." George careens back, slams into a wall, then crumples to the floor.)

GEORGE

Cranium!

MARY

You keep your voice down!

GEORGE

Busted it up!

MARY

You busted it up, George, not me!

GEORGE

I did?!

MARY

Just stay back!

GEORGE

Lip's all tingly.

MARY

It'll be more than tingly if you pull a stunt like that again.

GEORGE

Oh, I'll do more than pull a stunt, pretty lady. That tree's pure, see? Pure as the driven snow, whatever that means. So I'll pull a stunt! I'll pull those trink-a-links right offa her!

(George drives for the tree again. Mary winds up and smacks him hard once! Twice! And again, sending him flying back across the room.)

FREYA(O.S.)

Mama?! We hear bells! Is Santa here?!

LUKE(O.S.)

Santa's here?!

MARY

Santa's not here, children, I'm just—banging my pan, that's all! Now go to sleep!

GEORGE

Can't feel my face too good.

MARY

Get out.

GEORGE

Shattered my cheekbone. Hurts real bad.

MARY

I don't care anymore, George. I just want you to go.

> (Suddenly, from far off, we hear the unmistakable jingling of sleigh-bells, then ho-ho-hos. Santa's on his way.)

GEORGE

What's that? Who's there?

MARY

It's midnight. Oh, God, I didn't realize it had gotten so late.

GEORGE

Is that him? That's him, isn't it?

MARY

You can't be here, George, not tonight, not like this.

GEORGE

This is my <u>house</u>!

MARY

This is his night!

GEORGE

Not in here, it's not! Not in—Here he comes.

(We hear the jingly tread of boot-bells at the front door. Santa enters—a fearsome, avenging Santa.)

SANTA

(Gravely)

Merry Christmas.

MARY

Merry Christmas, Santa.

SANTA

(To George)

Get up.

MARY

Don't hurt him, Santa. Please.

GEORGE

You got some nerve, you know that?! Coming into my house in the middle of the night!

SANTA

Tonight I come and go as I please.

GEORGE

Tonight's a working night for you, is that it?

SANTA

That's right.

GEORGE

Got your list, do you?

SANTA

I always have my list.

GEORGE

I got MY list! Guess what?! You're on it! 'Cause I know what you do! At night! In other people's homes! You're the one who's naughty, see! NOT ME!!

(George charges. Santa, with super-human strength, grabs George, spins him around, and hurls him hard into the wall.)

MARY

Santa, please! He doesn't know what he's doing!

SANTA

He knows.

(George staggers to his feet.)

GEORGE

You know when I'm sleeping?! I know when YOU'RE sleeping!

SANTA

SLEEPING?!!

(Santa jingles his bells at George. George cries out, covers his ears, then collapses to the floor in agony.)

SANTA

I have not slept since The Creation! I am of the eternal! And now you shall feel my power!

(Santa lifts a massive gift box over his head, meaning to crush George with it. Freya and Luke appear in the doorway.)

FREYA

Santa?

LUKE

Santa?

(Startled, Santa drops the package on George. From here on out, Santa assumes his familiar, jolly demeanor when dealing with the children, but switches to grim and avenging when dealing with the adults.)

SANTA

Ho-ho-hello, children!

(The children run to Santa. He hugs them.)

FREYA

Did you bring us presents?

SANTA

I brought you one present—a kind of present.

MARY

Santa, please, they're not ready.

SANTA

They are ready. They will have to be ready.

(To Freya and Luke)

For I am your present, children. I—am your father! Ho ho ho ho ho ho ho ho—!

MARY

Stop!

SANTA

Ho ho—ho?!

MARY

For God's sake, the shame!

SANTA

There is no shame! So now the time has come for you to join me—at the North Pole.

FREYA

Father . . . Christmas?

SANTA

I'm tired of the lies, the once-a-year rendezvous, the tip-toeing around. No more! Get your things.

MARY

But . . . Mrs. Claus. I thought—

SANTA

I told her this morning.

GEORGE

Then she called me, you believe that?! On my cell phone! Still got it on the voice mail! Told me the whole story—the whole Story of Christmas!

Yeah, I been drinking ever since! And the way I figure it?! I ain't never gonna stop drinking!

SANTA
Indeed! Now how would you children like to ride in my sleigh tonight?

FREYA
Oh, boy!

LUKE
Oh, boy!
(Luke and Freya race off.)

GEORGE
Not that I didn't suspect. Those children, with their strange powers.

MARY
Don't you DARE talk about their powers!

GEORGE
And you, Mary, so cold. Always cold. Cold as Christmas.

MARY
I love him, George. And he loves me.

GEORGE
He "loves" you?! He can't love anybody! He loves everybody, so that means he loves nobody!

> (George charges, Santa holds up a finger, George convulses then collapses. Luke and Freya reenter wearing winter coats and carrying little suitcases.)

SANTA

Go outside now, children. And don't feed the reindeer, they have their own special food.

(The children race outside.)

SANTA

I'll wait for you in the Sleigh. Don't be long.

(Santa exits after Luke and Freya.)

MARY

Well, I suppose this is goodbye.

GEORGE

How long has this been going on?

MARY

George, please—

GEORGE

How long?!

MARY

Since the time of Zagmuth in ancient Mesopotamia. Since the rise of Saturnalia and the coming of Yule. For a thousand years—a thousand thousand years!

(She thinks)

Which is a million! A million years!

GEORGE

You're not that old!

MARY

You never really understood me, did you, George.

GEORGE

Not really.

MARY

I wasn't the first of his mortal consorts! But, so help me, I shall be his last!

GEORGE

(Accusatorially)

I have no idea what you're talking about!

MARY

Merry Christmas, George. Happy New Year.

(Mary exits. George calls after her.)

GEORGE

I don't understand you?! You don't understand me! What about my needs—my medical needs?! Cranium! Sternum's all splintered up! Can't breathe too good! What about those things, Mary, huh?! What about my cranium! Ow! Ouch! Cranium!

(Outside, we hear a whip, and then the Jingling of sleigh-bells. George slumps to the floor. We hear Santa outside fading into the distance as the lights fade to black.)

SANTA(O.S.)

On, Dasher! On, Dancer! Don't touch that, children! Mmmerry Christmas! Ho-ho-ho ... ! Mmmerry Christmas!

(Black out.) ☻

CEREMONIES THAT HAVE NOT RECRUDESCED BECAUSE WE NEVER SUCCEEDED IN GETTING RID OF THEM IN THE FIRST PLACE

BY P.J. O'ROURKE

Christmas

Christmas begins about the first of December with an office party and ends when you finally realize what you spent, around April fifteenth of the next year.

Christmas has replaced Lent as a period of penance. Christmas is when you punish yourself for having spent eleven months claiming to be friends with a pack of useless and nasty people you hardly know. Now you're forced to go out and buy each of them an expensive gift. In return you'll receive a dozen bottles of strawberry-flavored wine cooler and a pair of Louis Vuitton earmuffs.

There is a remarkable breakdown of taste and intelligence at Christmastime. Mature, responsible, grown men wear neckties made out of holly leaves and drink alcoholic beverages with raw egg yolks and cottage cheese in them. Otherwise reasonable adult women start hinting to their dates about emerald bracelets before they've even been French-kissed. The only thing that's even slightly interesting about Christmas is that office party. It's nice to see the people at work *admitting* that they're drunk and not getting anything done.

The worst part of Christmas is dinner with the family, when you realize how truly mutated and crippled is the gene stock from which you sprang.

It's customarily said that Christmas is done "for the kids." Considering how awful Christmas is and how little our society really likes children, this must be true.

Thanksgiving

Thanksgiving is a sort of trial run for Christmas, especially for Christmas dinner. Thanksgiving is when that mysterious large and tasteless animal (supposed to be a bird but more closely resembling a stewed beach ball) is first placed upon the table. This will be sliced apart and put on everyone's plate and then collected from the plates and put back together and served again at Christmas.

A number of other remarkable things show up in holiday dinners, such as "dressing," which is a loaf of bread that got hit by a truck full of animal innards, and pies made out of something called "mince," although if anyone has ever seen a mince in its natural state he did not live to tell about it.

Thanksgiving is so called because we are all thankful that it comes only once a year.

New Year's

The proper behavior all through the holiday season is to be drunk. This drunkenness culminates on New Year's Eve, when you get so drunk you kiss the person you're married to. The hangover begins the next day and lasts through Super Bowl Sunday, when you lose whatever money you had left from Christmas by betting on the Toronto Blue Jays, who are not even a football team. The rest of the holiday season is spent adding up bills.

LAST LAST CHANCE

BY FIONA MAAZEL

Sharon asks what I'm doing for New Year's, which is tonight. The Jewish New Year started months ago, but such is the tyranny of the Christian calendar. Naturally, I don't much like New Year's. In order from earliest to most recent, I have spent the last five like this: with people from boarding school at an unofficial reunion near school grounds watching the ball drop on TV; at some party having sex with some guy while watching the ball drop on TV; watching the ball drop on TV with syringe in tryst with a vein that showed itself, miraculously, just before midnight; at a rehab where we watched the ball drop with the sound off because Mandy was made psychotic by the din of any crowd; and finally, last year, in a network of lies disported to make all my friends think I was spending the night with other friends so that I could actually spend the night alone, watching the ball drop on TV.

"Watching the ball drop," I say.

"Oh no, you can't do that. The ball is evil. Bob Barker is evil."

I think she means Dick Clark.

"Dick, Bob, whatever. They dye their hair, they are evil."

"I didn't realize you felt so strongly about it."

"Well, I do. Come to my house. We're playing Twister. We'll ring in the New Year like a pile of puppies."

@ @ @

I decided to go with Wanda. We took her truck. She'd fried the clutch so bad, we couldn't get out of first gear.

"Your driving's making me sick," I said.

"Vomit in this car and you are dead."

We could see Sharon's five minutes before we got there. She had a glowing Santa on the lawn. Candy-cane torchlights. Mylar bows on every post. When we opened her door, it jingle-belled.

You're here, look who's here! She offered up two goblets of nog and some pinecone earrings. Everyone was wearing them, it seemed. Over her shoulder, I saw people I did not know sitting around a fire. Who are these people? "The brass," Wanda said, and arranged her face into a smile. The brass are the men who run ZOG chicken, and their wives. They were eating fruitcake.

Sharon took our coats. "The gang's over there," she said, and pointed to a room opposite the brass. "But I'm trying to get them to mingle."

Wanda said, "No problem," and cozied up to the dowager brass whose deceased had founded the plant.

I made for the gang. They were crowded around the TV, which had me relieved. I am a little superstitious about the ball. Still, there were three hours to go, so why the focus?

I was told to shush. If I hadn't been so drained of the wherewithal to interest myself in other people, I might have gauged the tone of the room sooner. As is, it took a few seconds to realize we were watching the TV with horror. It was an emergency news flash: The superplague had hit California. It had not traveled from Minnesota; this was a new outbreak. The nation's lunatic had struck again. Four people were dead.

The screen split into a quartet of coverage from the White House, the CDC's headquarters, the Pentagon, and the bio-containment facility where the four victims and their families were being held. We watched a series of speeches asking for calm. We listened to scientists admit the situation was grave. We saw footage of the moon men zipping across Carmel and Big Sur, rounding up anyone who might have come into contact with the victims. Consensus among the experts: If this gets to Los Angeles, we are doomed.

I held up my glass. "Nog, anyone?"

Rachel turned off the TV.

We heard laughter from the brass and envied it. Ten minutes ago, we were laughing, too.

Sharon burst through the door. She was a little drunk. Why the long faces? It's New Year's!

Without discussion, we were agreed not to spoil everyone else's night. There was nothing to be done. In fact, I almost wished the press would start vectoring the news as per the North Koreans, where so long as you're hidden, who cares if you're starving. Because really, what is the point? We can't protect ourselves, there's nowhere to run. Okay, so maybe some of us will finally begin to live each day as if it were our last. But as Wanda said, most of us can't finance our dreams, last day or not.

"Well, come on!" Sharon said. "We're setting up Twister."

We filed out of the room like men off the plank.

    💀   💀   💀

Twister for adults is made for reunion weekends in the log cabin, just you and your five best friends from college graduated twenty years ago today, look at our paths divergent, and yet here we are with a bottle of Chardonnay, six wounded hearts, and a slipped disk. The one with the disc gets bedridden. The others cancel the river raft. Tempers flare, resentments will out. There is inadvisable sex between two. There are tears in the chamomile. Convalescence, hangovers, s'mores. If only half as much happens tonight, it will bring the tramontane of Pennsylvania to their knees.

Because we are new to each other, Sharon has issued name cards. Linda and Kathleen. Deirdre, Noah, Lonna, Donna. We are like the ZOG family singers. Rachel shakes out the Twister mat and secures it to the floor with paperweights. Doug Guildenstein, homosexual son of dead founder brass, mans the spinner. He has a bad knee. He sits on the couch with legs crossed, spinner handy. Merlot on deck. He's wearing dress socks and penny loafers. Sharon seems alarmed by the prospect of brass v. yeomen, so she divides us up herself. She makes like she's assessing our skills and choosing accordingly. Half of us find this funny, mostly the brass. The eldest has an umlaut in her name. Urüla. No clue how you end up with a name like Urüla or whence the umlaut, but Joe says she's from New York, which apparently explains it.

Urüla wants to captain our team. She's got a vision. The youngest and most limber among us should go last. Seems reasonable enough, only the first trial asks Sal to make like a starfish and hold it. He does not last three seconds. He's nearing seventy. He is an accountant.

Urüla revisits her game plan. We are asked to huddle. I am beginning to wonder if she didn't used to be one of those Eastern Bloc gymnastic coaches.

Stanley and Wanda take to the mat. She's on all fours, he rides her like a pony. Half of us find this funny, mostly the yeomen. Doug trades his Merlot for brandy. Watching him fondle that snifter puts me in mind of *Masterpiece Theater*. He looks ready to impart wisdom. And when he calls out a new position, it sounds Shakespearean. Poor Doug, he was meant for better things. Had he not gambled away his share of ZOG stock, he might have financed a regional theater dedicated to the lost works of.

I am told to squat and loop my arm around Wanda's knee. Ah, the much touted indignity of Twister. I loop, Joe straddles, Kathleen assumes a yoga pose that seems unfair. She's had training. I bet she can give herself head.

Come Hannah's turn, the game gets ugly. Doug sends her to the other side of the mat, but somehow she's able to hook her foot around my ankle and effect a collapse that slams me into an elbow and splits my chin.

"Foul!" cries Urüla. "That's a foul!"

Doug reminds Urüla that there are no fouls in Twister. Shylock could not have said it better. The game takes a break. My chin trails blood across the mat. I wonder if premonitions of blood account for the mat's fabric, easily cleaned with sponge and water.

Stanley ministers to my chin, which is more flap than chin. Two flaps really. Must be some dry skin on Joe's elbow, dry like a rotary blade. Stanley cannot stanch the blood, so he has me lean way back in my chair. I can see up his nose. If his teeth were terrible, it'd be like a dental appointment. My dentist, anyway, has an ugly mouth. I figure in the way shrinks want to help you because they're crazy, dentists have the ugly mouth.

Hannah peers into my chin.

"How's the movie?" I ask.

"You'll need stitches. But probably I can sew you up for now."

"Why does that not excite me?"

"What if I used black string? What if I rounded you up some painkillers?"

Stanley says, "No way. It'll get infected. Plus, you're twelve." He looks at me. "She's twelve!"

"Well, what would you suggest? No way we're getting to an ER in this weather."

"Does it hurt?"

"Not if I get painkillers."

"We could tape it?"

Hannah rolls her eyes. "You think Scotch tape is a better idea than sewing it shut? You're a retard."

Sharon comes in to check on me. Takes one look at the gash and says "*Ewwww.*"

Does she have any disinfectant? No, but she has vodka. All those who think vodka's as good as hydrogen peroxide, say aye. It's a split vote.

Doug's snifter avails itself. Fits my chin perfectly. I dip and howl because fuck it hurts. Sharon produces Percocet and Advil. First easy choice I've had all day. Hannah cuts strips of cheesecloth left over from turkey dinner. She dresses my chin, tapes the cloth to my cheeks and secures the bandage by looping the rest of the cloth up over my head, much like a football player's chin guard, only I look post-surgery, and those guys look hot.

"Crisis averted!" Sharon says.

But Twister is done.

☠ ☠ ☠

I look at my watch. An hour to go. There's a small TV on the desk, which I turn on to check the progress of mayhem at Times Square. But all I get is Dick Clark musing on the dialectic before our very eyes, the unfettering of joy come the New Year vis-à-vis the unfettering of terror the rest of us are experiencing since this telecast is interrupted fifty times by news from the plague front where six have now perished alongside the decency of Californians jostling for supplies at Ace Hardware.

Stanley walks in and covers his eyes. "Turn it off! I can't watch."

"What's happening out there?"

He shrugs. "Looks like your chin stopped bleeding."

I twirl my finger in the air. "Did you hear I'm going to rehab tomorrow?"

"Yes. That's good."

I sit up, furious. "So you want me to go?"

"Oh, grow up, Lucy."

I slump back into his chest. "Why's it good again?"

He sighs. "It's going to be fine, you'll see."

"Hey look," I say, pointing at a board game. "There's Sorry. Let's play Sorry."

My spirits rally with the thought. I love this game, whose goal is to get all your pieces to the finish line, but whose pleasure is to screw as many of your opponents as possible along the way. It's a game of alliances and betrayal. You team up with a player to retard a third, then stab your teammate in the back. And you are encouraged to apologize for it. How many board games actually thrive on sarcasm? And how many players have been known to cut loose with a rapacity that belies good character? I bet this game chips away at ZOG solidarity. I bet the executive board dissolves next week. "Let's play!" I say, and grab Stanley's arm.

"Sorry? That game's for ten-year-olds."

And like that I start to cry.

"Oh, honey, I didn't mean it. We can play Sorry."

I dump my head in a pillow. I say I hate rehab, that I'm scared of the plague, that this heartache is unsustainable—I miss Eric so much, I have no one to talk to—but the sobs are censoring and Stanley gets none of it.

"Is it your chin? Does it hurt?"

He strokes my hair, which makes me cry all the more.

"I know baby," he says. "I know. It's gonna be okay. Let's get you some nog."

It's nearing midnight. Group talk has devolved into accounts of everyone's happiest moment. Or top five. But because we are drunk, nostalgia quickly cedes to gloom. Five happy moments. Some of us have to dig deep to produce three. And even then, they are so far in the past as to offer no comfort.

Rachel lifts her glass. "To the year of living dangerously," she says.

The brass hear, hear. The yeomen nod.

"I saw that movie," Noah says. "There was some little Asian lady in it, right?"

"To the year of happy moments!" Sharon says.

Grunts all around.

"To the year of sex!" Doug says.

We glance at his mother, but she's ten sheets to the wind.

"To sex on the pool table!" Rachel shouts.

Kathleen stands and raises her glass. "To sex with yourself," she says gravely.

I knew it!

By now, everyone is laughing. Even Hannah, though she's still sore about the thread.

I put up my hands and wait for quiet. I want to toast something I've had just once. And I want to honor the inexperience that makes me think it can't last. I raise my glass and notice I've been drinking rum, which is foul. "To sex with the one you love," I say, and drain the last of it.

My toast is met with appreciation until Hannah lets out a snort and with it, a wad of gum. Her laughter is picked up by Linda, who, between gasps says, "I'm sorry, that was very sweet, it's just that you standing there with that bandage and—" She gets no further.

Just as well since here comes the countdown. Sharon is determined to use her watch, despite Kathleen's thrusting her GPS timepiece in Sharon's face. With a minute to go, the brass gather around Kathleen while the rest of us stick with Sharon. This is her worst nightmare. Our countdown is symbolic of the class divide that scuttles ambitions like peace on earth. Our countdown is syncopated. The brass hug and kiss a whole five seconds before we do.

"Well, that settles it," I say. "My year is ruined." 💀

OH, CHRISTMAS TREE

BY AUGUSTEN BURROUGHS

Natalie and I are in the mangy TV room watching *The Love Boat*. We've dragged the wing chairs up on either side of the Christmas tree and are reaching over to pick through its branches in pursuit of any candy canes that remain. Most of them have already been eaten. By accident, Natalie stuck a plastic one in her mouth. Why Agnes insists on mixing plastic candy canes with the real ones is beyond both of us.

I should mention that it's May.

Most of the needles have fallen off the tree and are now carpeting the floor and have been tracked throughout the house. Everyone has brown, sharp little needles in their beds. The branches are dry and crispy and tend to snap off when you tug at them.

I absently pull at a branch until it snaps. Julie, the cruise director, suggests to a clinically depressed passenger that the aft deck is a fine place to meet new people, recover from a failed love affair, and I let the branch fall on the floor with the others.

Our lives are one endless stretch of misery punctuated by processed fast foods and the occasional crisis or amusing curiosity.

The fact that the Christmas tree is still standing five months after Christmas is extremely disturbing to everyone in the house. But we all feel someone else should be the one to remove it. It is somebody else's responsibility. And in most everyone's mind, that somebody is Agnes.

But Agnes has refused to move the tree. "I'm not your slave," she has screamed again and again. She will straighten her Virgin Mary candles on the sideboard, sweep the carpets, wash the occasional pot, but she will not touch this tree.

"Personally, I don't give a fuck if this tree stays here forever. I'm used to it now," Natalie states as she stares straight ahead at the TV. "I hope it does stay up forever. It'll teach Agnes a lesson."

I don't really care if it stays up forever, either. It fits perfectly with the rest of the house. It's kind of like dust. There seems to be a certain amount of dust that will collect on the surface of things and then no more. The house is already such a hodgepodge of strangeness that the tree is not out of place.

Besides, I have experience with a misplaced Christmas tree in my past.

💀 💀 💀

I was ten and all winter my mother and father had been screaming at each other. My brother had moved out of the house to live with members of his rock band, so I was trapped alone with my parents. There was a Christmas calendar on the refrigerator, the kind with little doors that you open one day at a time until the big day, December twenty-fifth. I would sit on the floor in front of the refrigerator opening the doors and wishing I could crawl inside one of those warm, glittering rooms.

"You goddamn son of a bitch," my mother screamed at the top of her lungs. "You want me to be your damn mother? Well I am not your damn mother. You are in love with that woman, you sick bastard."

"Jesus Christ, Deirdre. Would you please calm down. You're hysterical."

"I most certainly am *not* hysterical," my mother screamed, utterly hysterical.

It went on like this all winter. Snow piled on the deck railings outside and the house grew darker as the bows of the pine trees leaned against the windows, heavy with snow.

My father spent as much time as he could downstairs in their bedroom drinking. And my mother channeled her energy into a manic holiday frenzy.

She played one song on one album again and again: "We Need A Little Christmas" from *Mame*. When the song would end, my mother would set down the bowl of cranberries she was threading for the tree and place the needle back at the beginning.

She set red and green candles out on the teak dining table, and placed the Norwegian nutcracker in the center of a bowl of pecans from her father's orchard in Georgia. She dragged her Singer sewing machine out of the basement and began making Christmas stockings, angels and reindeer ornaments for the tree.

When I suggested cookies, she baked fourteen batches.

She read me Christmas stories, sketched a Christmas card with pen and ink and had it printed to send to family and friends, and she even let the dog sleep on the sofa during the day.

Her sudden and feverish intensity of cheer transferred onto me. And I became obsessed with decorating my room in the spirit of Christmas. Specifically, I wanted my room to look like one of the displays at the mall. While my mother was tasteful and restrained, I filled my room with multiple strands of cheap blinking lights. They hung from the ceiling and dripped from my window and walls. I wrapped thick ropes of gaudy silver garland around my desk lamp, my bookshelf and around my mirror. I spent my allowance on two blinking stars that I hung on either side of my closet door. It was as if I had become infected with a virus of bad taste.

My mother insisted on the largest tree we could find at the Christmas tree farm. It had to be removed from the ground with a chain saw and then carried to the car by two burly men. When they roped it to the top of the Aspen, the car sank.

At home, the tree nearly reached the top of our seventeen-foot ceiling. And it was nearly as wide as the sofa.

My mother had it completely decorated in a matter of hours. There were balls nestled deep in the branches, silver bells placed above gold ribbons. It had everything, including popcorn and cranberry garlands she had hand-strung while watching *The Jeffersons.*

"Isn't this festive?" she asked, sweating profusely.

I nodded.

"We're going to make this a special Christmas. Even if your goddamn sonofabitch father can't bring himself to do anything but raise a glass to his lips."

She began to sing along with Angela Lansbury's warbling about dragging out the holly and throwing up the tree before my mood crashes and I want to kill myself, or however it went.

Two days before Christmas my brother came home. He was his usual, sullen self and when my mother asked him if he planned on staying for Christmas, he grunted and replied, "I don't know."

I, myself, had my own doubts about the coming holiday. Although there were already dozens of presents beneath the tree, I had not noticed a single one in the shape of the gift I most wanted: Tony Orlando and Dawn's *Tie a Yellow Ribbon 'Round the Old Oak Tree.* If I did not get this album, I had no reason to live. And yet there was nothing flat and square under the tree. There were plenty of puffy things—sweaters, shirts with built-in vests, the bell-bottom polyester slacks I loved, maybe a pair of platform shoes—but without that record, there might as well be no Christmas.

My mother must have sensed my feelings.

Because that evening, when my father came upstairs and made a comment about all the pine needles stuck in the carpet, my mother's brain chemistry mutated.

"Well, if that's the way everybody feels," she screamed, running into the living room, her blue Marimekko caftan flowing behind her, "then we'll just call the whole damn thing off."

I was astonished by her physical strength. What had taken two large men many minutes of concentrated effort to hoist on top of our brown station wagon, my mother was able to topple in a matter of seconds.

Tinsel, shattered Christmas balls and lights were smeared across the floor as she dragged the thing through the living room, out the deck door and straight over the edge.

I'd never seen such a display of physical strength from her before and I was impressed.

My brother snickered. "What's the matter with her?"

My father was angry. "Your damn mother's crazy is what's the matter."

My mother stormed back inside the house and swiped the needle off the record. She leaned over and began rummaging through the wooden captain's trunk where she kept her albums. When she found the record she was looking for, she placed it on the stereo, turned the volume up full blast and set the needle down.

I am woman hear me roar in numbers too big to ignore . . .

Hope comes into the TV room. "There anything left?" she says, pointing to the tree, meaning food.

"No," Natalie says, stuffing the bend of a candy cane in her mouth. "This is the last one."

"It figures," she says and walks away.

"I'm depressed now," Natalie says. "And fat."

Poo comes into the room. He goes to the tree looking for a snack. The tree has become the new refrigerator. Miraculously, he finds a chocolate Santa head in the back. How did it escape? He peels away the foil and pops it in his mouth. "What's up?" he says.

"Nothing," Natalie says, staring straight ahead at the TV.

Julie cracks a joke on TV and several of the passengers laugh.

Poo says, "You guys are boring," and goes away.

Hope comes back into the room, angry. "You know," she begins, "since you guys spend the most time in here, I really think you should take care of this tree problem."

We both turn and stare at her.

"Well, I do," she says.

Natalie says, "You want the Christmas tree out of here?"

"Yes. It's May, for crying out loud."

Natalie stands and reaches for the base of the tree. In one swift motion she yanks and the tree falls. Wordlessly, she drags the tree through the doorway down the hall and crams it into Hope's bedroom.

"Don't you dare do that, Natalie," Hope shouts.

But Natalie has done it. "Now it's your fucking problem."

As Natalie heads up the stairs Hope shouts after her, "If that's how you feel, maybe we shouldn't even have a Christmas this year. Maybe we should just cancel it."

I walk into the living room and sit at the piano to play the single song I know: "The Theme from *The Exorcist*."

☠ ☠ ☠

That evening, the tree has found its way into the dining room. It is on its side beneath the bay window. Agnes is in the dining room with her broom, hunched over sweeping. She sweeps around the tree. She sweeps for hours. She sweeps until at sometime after midnight Hope comes into the room, groggy. "Jesus, Agnes. I'm trying to sleep. Do you have to make such a racket?"

"Somebody's got to stay on top of things in this house," she says. "I'm just trying to hold it all together."

"Well, would you mind holding it all together in the morning? I need to be at Dad's office early."

"Just go back to sleep. I'm hardly making any noise at all."

"It's all your humming," Hope says. "At least stop that."

"I'm not humming."

"Yes you are, Agnes. I can hear you clean through the wall into my room. You're humming that damn 'Jingle Bells.' Jeepers, it's not even Christmas." Hope turns and goes back to her room.

Agnes resumes sweeping. "I wasn't humming," she mutters to her-self. "These crazy kids."

💀 💀 💀

The next morning as I look at the discarded tree, I am reminded of a turkey carcass. For some reason, Christmas trees and poultry bones have a difficult time finding their way out of this house.

Preparation for Thanksgiving may be an intense and focused event at this house, but the cleanup is not. It's interesting that Natalie will go without sleep for two days straight; she will clean the entire house with a scrub brush; she will single-handedly prepare a feast for twenty; she will do all this without a murmur of complaint. But afterward, the dishes and pots and pans will remain unwashed for weeks. The turkey itself, now just cage of bones, will be passed from room to room. It is not uncom-mon to see the turkey bones sitting on top of the television set one day and in the bathroom under the sink another. But never, ever will you see it in the trash.

I have found wishbones in that house that predate the Nixon admin-istration. And drumsticks that could quite possibly be of interest to archaeologists.

Eventually, the pans will be washed, the glasses returned to their roach-infested cabinets, and the silverware scrubbed free of debris. But Christmas trees and turkey bones tend to stay awhile. 💀

KEEPING CHRISTMAS IN YOUR HEART ALL YEAR LONG

BY ALYSIA GRAY PAINTER

January 18—Deck the house in lots of bright, flashing lights, oversize reindeer, and holiday gewgaws. An aural touch, such as continuous carols playing out the front window, will keep the neighbors in good humor.

February 3—Wish five strangers Merry Christmas today. Repeat "Merry Christmas" joyfully when they ask you to repeat what you just said. Hugs are nice here.

March 11—Build a snowman. If no snow is available, use whatever fetid earth you can scrape up, or any old milk cartons/newspapers lying around. Kids'll love it.

May 30—Set up a hot nog stand out by the city pool. Ask parents if little fishes can have a sprinkle of nutmeg in their cups first. Do not let yourself be snapped by a wet towel while handling the scalding beverage.

June 20—Visit the mall Santa. If he isn't there, be Santa yourself, inviting strangers to sit in your lap. Listen well but promise nothing.

July 4—Explode some holly, making sure it is tinder dry and crackly. See the pretty fire colors. The firemen will be merrily wearing festive red or yellow when they arrive. Have cookies ready!

August 8—Gift tag Popsicles.

September 1–30—Repeatedly ask same neighbor for cup of whiskey for world-famous St. Nick Nuggets. When he first refuses, jump in the leaf pile in his yard, yelling "Santa's comin' in for a landing," or something fun like that. Living next to a card such as yourself may not raise the value of your neighbors' house, but it is sure to raise the value of their hearts.

October 31—Upon opening door for trick-or-treaters, guess each child's costume as Blitzen or Comet. Then hand out candy canes to disappointed goblins with a "Ho-Ho-Halloween wishes" or similar.

November 29—Put roast turkey in makeshift manger, pray. Bread stuffing and cranberry salad artfully placed make for fine cattle and sheep.

December 25—Vow to keep Christmas all next year, or at least every other Thursday, preferably between seven and eight in the evening. Devote the rest of the coming months to keeping National Poultry day in your heart. Watch for coming tips and hints. ☺

CHRISTMAS MEANS GIVING

BY DAVID SEDARIS

For the first twelve years of our marriage Beth and I happily set the neighborhood standard for comfort and luxury. It was an established fact that we were brighter and more successful but the community seemed to accept our superiority without much complaint and life flowed on the way it should. I used to own a hedge polisher, an electric shovel, and three Rolex gas grills that stood side by side in the backyard. One was for chicken, one for beef, and the third I had specially equipped to steam the oriental pancakes we were always so fond of. When the holidays rolled around I used to rent a moving van and drive into the city, snatching up every bright new extravagance that caught my eye. Our twin sons, Taylor and Weston, could always count on the latest electronic toy or piece of sporting equipment. Beth might receive a riding vacuum cleaner or a couple pair of fur-lined jeans and those were just the stocking stuffers! There were disposable boats, ultrasuede basketballs, pewter knapsacks, and solar-powered card shufflers. I'd buy them shoes and clothes and bucketfuls of jewelry from the finest boutiques and department stores. Far be it from me to snoop around for a bargain or discount. I always paid top dollar, thinking that those foot-long price tags really *meant* something about Christmas. After opening our gifts we'd sit down to a sumptuous banquet, feasting on every imaginable variety of meat and pudding. When one of us got full and felt uncomfortable, we'd stick a silver wand down our throats, throw up, and start eating all over again. In effect, we weren't much different from anyone else. Christmas was a season of bounty and, to the outside world, we were just about the most bountiful people anyone could think of. We thought we were happy but that all changed on one crisp Thanksgiving day shortly after the Cottinghams arrived.

If my memory serves me correctly, the Cottinghams were trouble from the very first moment they moved in next door. Doug, Nancy, and their unattractive eight-year-old daughter, Eileen, were exceedingly envious and greedy people. Their place was a little smaller than ours but it made sense, seeing as there were four of us and only three of them. Still though, something about the size of our house so bothered them that they hadn't even unpacked the first suitcase before starting construction on an indoor skating rink and a three-thousand-square-foot pavilion where Doug could show off his collection of pre-Columbian sofa beds. Because we felt like doing so, Beth and I then began construction on an indoor soccer field and a five-thousand-square-foot rotunda where I could comfortably display *my* collection of pre-*pre*-Columbian sofa beds. Doug would tell all the neighbors I'd stolen the idea from him but I'd been thinking about pre-pre-Columbian sofa beds long before the Cottinghams pulled into town. They just had to cause trouble, no matter what the cost. When Beth and I built a seven-screen multiplex theatre they had to go and build themselves a *twelve*-screener. This went on and on and, to make a long story short, within a year's time neither of us had much of a yard. The two houses now butted right up against each other and we blocked out the west-side windows so that we wouldn't have to look into their gaudy fitness center or second-story rifle range.

Despite their competitive nature, Beth and I tried our best to be neighborly and occasionally invite them over for rooftop barbecues and so forth. I'd attempt to make adult conversation, saying something like "I just paid eight thousand dollars for a pair of sandals that don't even fit me." Doug would counter, saying that he himself had just paid ten thousand for a single flip-flop he wouldn't wear even if it *did* fit him. He was always very combative that way. If it cost you seventy thousand dollars to have a cavity filled, you could bet your boots it cost him at least a hundred and twenty-five thousand. I suffered his company for the better part of a year until one November evening when we got into a spat over which family sent out the most meaningful Christmas card. Beth and I normally hired a noted photographer to snap a portrait of the entire family surrounded by the gifts we had received the year before. Inside the card would be the price of these gifts along with the message "Christmas Means Giving." The Cottinghams favored *their* card, which consisted of a Xeroxed copy of Doug and Nancy's stock portfolio. I said that while it is all very well and good to *have* money, their card said nothing about the way they *spent* money. Like our card said, Christmas means giving and even if he were to gussy up his stock report with a couple of press-on candy canes it would still fail to send the proper holiday message. The conversation grew quite heated and some punches were thrown between the wives. We'd all had a few drinks and by the time the Cottinghams left our house it was generally assumed that our friendship was over. I dwelled upon the incident for a day or two and then turned my attention toward the approaching holidays.

We'd just finished another of our gut-busting Thanksgiving dinners and Beth, the boys, and I were all watching a bullfight on TV. We could watch whatever we wanted back then because we still had our satellite dish. Juan Carlos Ponce de Velasquez had just been gored something fierce and we were all acting pretty excited about it when the doorbell rang. I figured one of the boys had ordered a pizza and opened the door surprised to find a foul-smelling beggar. He was a thin, barefooted man with pepperoni-sized scabs on his legs and an unkempt beard smeared with several different varieties of jam. I sensed it was the jam that we'd thrown into the garbage the night before and one look at our overturned trash can told me I was right. This had me pretty ticked off but before I could say anything abut it, the old bum pulled out a coffee mug and starting whining for money.

When Beth asked who was at the door I called out, "Code Blue," which was our secret signal that one of us should release the hounds. We had two of them back then, big Dobermans named Butterscotch and Mr. Lewis. Beth tried to summon them from the dining room but, having gorged themselves on turkey and stuffing, it was all they could do to lift their heads and vomit. Seeing as they were laid up, I got down on my hands and knees and bit the guy myself. Maybe it was the bull-fight but, for whatever reason, I had a sudden taste for blood. My teeth barely broke the skin but that was all it took to send the old coot hobbling over to the Cottinghams' place. I watched him pound upon their door, knowing full well what would happen when he told competitive Doug Copy Cat that I'd given him one measly bite on the calf. Beth called me into the house for one reason or another and when I returned to the door a few minutes later, I saw Helvetica, the Cottinghams' maid, taking a photograph of Doug, Nancy, and Eileen handing the tramp a one-dollar bill.

I knew something was up and, sure enough, two weeks later I came to find the exact same snapshot on the Cottinghams' Christmas card along with the words "Christmas means giving." That had always been *our* slogan and here he'd stolen it, twisting the message in an attempt to make us appear selfish. It had never been our way to give to others but I starting having second thoughts when I noticed the phenomenal response the Cottinghams received on the basis of their Christmas card. Suddenly they were all anyone was talking about. Walk into any holiday party and you'd hear, "Did you see it? I think it's positively enchanting. Here these people donated money to an absolute stranger! Can you beat that? A whole dollar they gave to this vagrant person with absolutely nothing to his name. If you ask me, those Cottinghams are a couple of very brave and generous people."

Doug would probably say that I unfairly stole his idea when I myself became a generous person but this was not the case. I'd been thinking of being generous long before he showed up on the scene and, besides that, if he could illegally pinch my holiday slogan, why couldn't I casually borrow a concept that had been around for a good ten years? When I first told people that I had given two dollars to the Inner City Headache Fund they turned away as if they didn't believe me. Then I actually *did* give two dollars to the Headache Fund and boy, did things ever change once I started flashing around that canceled check! Generosity can actually make people feel quite uncomfortable if you talk about it enough. I don't mean the bad "boring uncomfortable" but something much richer. If practiced correctly, generosity can induce feelings of shame, inadequacy, and even envy, to name just a few. The most important thing is that you keep some written or visual proof of your donation, otherwise there's really no point in giving to charity. Doug Cottingham would say I took that line from him but I'm pretty sure I read it in a tax manual.

I carried my canceled check to all the important holiday parties but people lost interest shortly after New Year's Eve. The season passed and I forgot all about my generosity until the following Thanksgiving, when the old tramp retuned to our neighborhood. He must have remembered the previous year's bite to the leg and, as a result, he was just about to pass us by when we called him in for a good dose of benevolence. First we videotaped him eating a palmful of leftover stuffing and then I had Beth snap a picture as I handed the geezer a VCR. It was an old top-loading Betamax but put a new cord on it and I'm sure it would have worked just fine. We watched then as he strapped it on his back and headed next door to continue his begging. The sight of that VCR was all it took for that skunk Doug Cottingham, who stepped into his house and returned to present the old codger with an eight-track tape deck and, oh, once again their maid was on hand to take a picture of it. We then called the tramp over to our house and gave him a year-old blow-dryer. The Cottinghams responded with a toaster oven. Within an hour we had advanced to pool tables and StairMasters. Doug gave him a golf cart and I gave him my satellite dish. This accelerated until any fool could see exactly where it was heading. Handing over the keys to his custom-built motorized travel sauna, Doug Cottingham gave me a look that seemed to say, "Top *that*, Neighbor!" Beth and I had seen that look before and we hated it. I could have easily topped his travel sauna but we were running low on film and thought it best to cut to the chase. Why needlessly escalate when we all knew what was most important? After a brief conference, Beth and I called the tramp back over and asked which he liked better, young boys or young girls. Much to our delight he said that girls were too much of a headache but that he'd had some fun with boys before his last visit to our local state penitentiary. That said, we gave him our ten-year-old sons, Taylor and Weston. Top that, Neighbor! You should have seen the look on Doug Cottingham's face! That year's Christmas card was the most meaningful to date. It pictured our sons' tearful good-bye along with the message "Christmas means giving until it hurts."

We were the toast of the neighborhood that holiday season, back on top where we belonged. Beth and I were *the* couple to have at any cocktail party or informal tree trimming.

"Where are those super generous people with that delightful Christmas card?" someone would ask, and the host would point in our direction while the Cottinghams bitterly gritted their teeth. As a last-ditch effort to better their names they donated their horse-faced daughter, Eileen, to a crew of needy pirates but anyone in the know could see it as the desperate gesture it really was. Once again we were the ones everyone wanted to be with and the warm glow of their admiration carried us through the holiday season. We received a second helping of awe early the following summer when the boys were discovered dead in what used to be Doug Cottingham's motorized travel sauna. The neighbors all wanted to send flowers but we said we'd prefer them to make a donation in our name to the National Sauna Advisory Board or the Sex Offenders Defense Fund. This was a good move and soon we had established ourselves as

"Christlike." The Cottinghams were, of course, furious and immediately set to work on their tired game of one-upsmanship. It was most likely the only thing they thought about but we didn't lose any sleep over it.

For that year's holiday cards we had settled on the theme "Christmas means giving until it bleeds." Shortly after Thanksgiving Beth and I had visited our local blood bank, where we nearly drained our bodies' precious accounts. Pale and dizzy from our efforts, it was all we could do to lift a hand and wave to one another from our respective gurneys. We recovered in time and were just sealing our envelopes when the postman delivered our neighbors' holiday card, which read "Christmas means giving of yourself." The cover pictured Doug lying outstretched upon an operating table as a team of surgeons busily, studiously, removed his glistening Cottingham lung. Inside the card was a photograph of the organ's recipient, a haggard coal miner holding a sign that read "Douglas Cottingham saved my life."

How dare he! Beth and I had practically invented the theme of medical generosity and it drove us mad, that smug, superior expression seeping from beneath our neighbor's surgical mask. Any long-married couple can, in times of crisis, communicate without speaking. This fact was illustrated as my wife and I wordlessly leapt into action. Throwing down her half-sealed envelope, Beth called the hospital while I contacted a photographer from our car phone. Arrangements were made and before the night was over I had donated both my eyes, a lung, one of my kidneys, and several important veins surrounding my heart. Having an unnatural attachment to her internal organs, Beth surrendered her scalp, her teeth, her right leg, and both breasts. It wasn't until after her surgery that we realized my wife's contributions were nontransferable, but by that time it was too late to sew them back on. She gave the scalp to a startled cancer patient, made a keepsake necklace of her teeth, and brought the leg and breasts to the animal shelter, where they were hand-fed to a litter of starving Border collies. That made the local evening news and once again the Cottinghams were green with envy over our good fortune. Donating organs to humans was one thing, but the community went wild over what Beth had done for those poor abandoned puppies. At each and every holiday party our hosts would beg my wife to shake their dog's hand or pass a blessing over the shell of their ailing tortoise. The coal-mining recipient of Doug Cottingham's lung had died when his cigarette set fire to the sheets and bandages covering his chest and now their name was practically worthless.

We were at the Hepplewhites' Christmas Eve party when I overheard Beth whisper, "That Doug Cottingham couldn't even donate a decent lung!" She laughed then, long and hard, and I placed my hand upon her shoulder, feeling the gentle bite of her keepsake necklace. I was no doubt drawing a good deal of attention to myself, but this was Beth's night and I gave it to her freely because I was such a generous person. We were a team, she and I, and while I couldn't see the way people were looking at us, I could feel it just as surely as I sensed the warmth cast off by the Hepplewhites' roaring fire.

There would be other Christmases, but I think Beth and I both knew that this one was special. In a year's time we would give away the house, our money, and what remained of our possessions. After scouting around for the right neighborhood, we would move into a village of cardboard boxes located beneath the Ragsdale Cloverleaf. The Cottinghams, true to their nature, would move into a smaller box next door. The begging would go relatively well during the holiday season but come deep winter things would get hard and we'd be visited by wave after wave of sorrow and disease. Beth would die after a long, sad struggle with tuberculosis but not until after Doug Cottingham and his wife had been killed by pneumonia. I'd try not to let it bother me that they had died first but in truth I would have a very difficult time dealing with it. Whenever my jealousy would get the best of me I would reflect back upon that perfect Christmas Eve at the Hepplewhites'. Shuddering beneath my blanket of damp newspapers, I'd try to recall the comforting sound of Beth's carefree laughter and picture her raw head thrown back in merriment, those bright, gleaming gums reflecting the light of a crystal chandelier. With luck, the memory of our love and generosity would lull me toward a profound and heavy sleep that would last until morning. ☙

NOTES ON CONTRIBUTORS

Jonathan Ames is the author of eight books, including *Wake Up, Sir!* and *The Double Life Is Twice As Good*. He is the creator of the new HBO series, "Bored to Death" and the winner of a Guggenheim Fellowship.

Dave Barry is a humor columnist whose work has appeared in more than five hundred newspapers in the United States and abroad. In 1988, he won the Pulitzer Prize for Commentary. Many people are still trying to figure out how this happened. Dave has also written a total of thirty books, although virtually none of them contain useful information. In his spare time, Dave is a candidate for president of the United States. Dave lives in Miami, Florida, with his wife, Michelle, a sportswriter. He has a son, Rob, and a daughter, Sophie, neither of whom thinks he's funny. The fourth book in his *Peter and the Starcatchers* series was published in fall of 2009.

Robert Benchley (1889–1945), one of the original members of the Algonquin Round Table, was an American humorist best known for penning essays and articles for *Life*, *Vanity Fair* and the *New Yorker*. In 1935, he won an Academy Award for his short film *How to Sleep*.

Roy Blount Jr.'s books include *Alphabet Juice*, *Long Time Leaving*, and *Be Sweet: A Conditional Love Story*. He is a panelist on NPR's "Wait, Wait... Don't Tell Me," a columnist for the *Oxford American*, a member of the Fellowship of Southern Writers, and president of the Authors Guild.

Daniel Blythe was born in Maidstone, UK, in 1969. He is the author of ten books, including the acclaimed novels *The Cut*, *Losing Faith*, *This Is The Day*, and the bestselling *Encyclopaedia Of Classic '80s Pop*. He has

also written the irreverent politics primer *X Marks The Box*, to be published when the General Election is called (2009 or 2010) and the new
Doctor Who novel *Autonomy*. Daniel lives on the edge of Sheffield with
his wife and their two young children.

Charles Bukowski is one of America's best-known contemporary writers
of poetry and prose. He was born in Andernach, Germany, and raised in
Los Angeles, where he lived for fifty years. He published his first story
in 1944, when he was twenty-four, and began writing poetry at the age of
thirty-five. He died in San Pedro, California, on March 9, 1994, at the age
of seventy-three, shortly after completing his last novel, *Pulp*.

Augusten Burroughs is the author of *Running with Scissors, Dry, Magical
Thinking: True Stories, Possible Side Effects,* and *A Wolf at the Table*.
Augusten's writing has appeared in numerous magazines and news-
papers around the world including the *New York Times* and *New York
Magazine*. He resides in New York City and western Massachusetts.

John Cheever (1912–1982) is the author of seven collections of stories
and five novels. He won the National Book Award for his first novel,
The Wapshot Chronicle, and in 1978 he received the National Book Critics
Circle Award and the Pulitzer Prize for *The Stories of John Cheever*. Shortly
before his death he was awarded the National Medal for Literature.

Billy Collins is the author of eight collections of poetry, including
*Ballistics, The Trouble with Poetry, Nine Horses, Sailing Alone Around the
Room, Questions About Angels, The Art of Drowning,* and *Picnic, Lightning*.
He is also the editor of *Poetry 180: A Turning Back to Poetry* and *180 More:
Extraordinary Poems for Every Day*. A distinguished professor of English
at Lehman College of the City University of New York, he was Poet
Laureate of the United States from 2001 to 2003 and Poet Laureate of
New York State from 2004 to 2006.

Corey Ford (1902–1969) attended Columbia University, where he was editor of the college humor magazine, the *Columbia Jester*. He began his literary career while still an undergraduate, selling stories and articles to such popular magazines as *Vanity Fair* and *Saturday Evening Post*. He named the *New Yorker* symbol Eustace Tilley and sat in on some Algonquin Round Table sessions. Some of his early books, written in parody form, were published under a pseudonym, "John Riddell." In all, Ford published more than thirty books during his lifetime, and over five hundred articles and short stories. "How to Guess Your Age" (1950) was widely plagiarized and may be circulating virally on the internet today.

Scott Horton is a contributing editor of *Harper's Magazine*. A New York attorney known for his work in emerging markets and international law, especially human rights law and the law of armed conflict, Horton lectures at Columbia Law School. A life-long human rights advocate, Scott is a member of the board of the National Institute of Military Justice, the Andrei Sakharov Foundation, the EurasiaGroup, and the American Branch of the International Law Association.

Greg Kotis wrote the book and cowrote the lyrics for *Urinetown: The Musical*. Other plays include *Jobey and Katherine, Eat the Taste, Pig Farm*, and *Yeast Nation*. Greg grew up in Wellfleet, Massachusetts, and now lives in Brooklyn with his daughter, India, his son, Milo, and his wife, Ayun Halliday.

Lewis Lapham is the editor of *Lapham's Quarterly*, the National Correspondent for *Harper's Magazine*, and the author of thirteen books, among them *Money and Class in America, The Wish for Kings, Theater of War*, and, most recently, *Pretensions to Empire*. For Bloomberg Radio he hosts a weekly program, "The World in Time." A member of the Council on Foreign Relations, he was inducted into the American Society of Magazine Editor's Hall of Fame in 2007. He lives in New York City.

Fiona Maazel is a writer and freelance editor. Her work has appeared in *Anthem, Bomb,* the *Mississippi Review,* the *New York Times,* N+1.com, *Pierogi Press, Salon, Tin House,* the *Village Voice,* and the *Yale Review.* She is a 2005 recipient of a Lannon Foundation Fellowship, winner of the Bard Prize for 2009, and a National Book Foundation "5 Under 35" honoree for 2008. She lives in Brooklyn, New York, and is currently at work on novel number two.

The author of seven novels and two collections of essays on wine, **Jay McInerney** is a regular contributor to *New York,* the *New York Times Book Review,* the *Independent,* and *Corriere della Sera.* His short fiction has appeared in the *New Yorker, Esquire, Playboy,* and *Granta.* In 2006, *Time* cited his 1984 debut, *Bright Lights, Big City,* as one of nine generation-defining novels of the twentieth century. He was the recipient of the 2006 James Beard Foundation's M.F.K. Fisher Distinguished Writing Award, and his novel *The Good Life* received the Grand Prix Littéraire de Deauville in 2007. "The Madonna of Turkey Season" appears in his most recent collection of stories, *How It Ended,* which was published by Alfred A. Knopf in 2009. He lives in Manhattan and in Bridgehampton, New York.

P.J. O'Rourke is a contributing editor at the *Weekly Standard,* an H.L. Mencken Fellow at the Cato Institute, and the author of thirteen books including, most recently, *Driving Like Crazy.*

Alysia Gray Painter lives in Los Angeles. Other work of hers has appeared in *McSweeney's Created in Darkness by Troubled Americans, McSweeney's Mountain Man Dance Moves, 101 Damnations, More Mirth of a Nation, May Contain Nuts,* the Modern Humorist web site, and books from the *Bark* magazine. She writes about tiny soaps, monogrammed bathrobes, and poolside daiquiris at www.hotelmemore.com.

S.J. Perelman (1904–1979) was born in Brooklyn, but grew up in Providence, Rhode Island. He attended Brown University where he drew cartoons for the school magazine. For over four decades his humorous short essays appeared frequently in the *New Yorker*. He contributed to the screenplays of *Animal Crackers* and *Horse Feathers* (and was a good friend of the Marx Brothers) and won an Oscar for the screenplay to *Around the World in 80 Days*. He was cocreator of the Broadway smash *One Touch of Venus*. "Waiting for Santy" is taken from *Most of the Most of S.J. Perelman*.

George Plimpton, a founding editor of the *Paris Review*, is the author or editor of more than thirty-five books, including *Paper Lion*, *Shadow Box*, *The Curious Case of Sidd Finch*, and *Edie*. He was appointed a Chevalier of the Legion D'Honneur, and in 2002 was made a member of the American Academy of Arts and Letters. He was also the honorary Fireworks Commissioner of New York City. He died in 2003.

A difficult day turns into great material for writer **Chris Radant**. In today's upside down world, with its population in a snit, Chris is up to her eye-balls with material and piles of undecipherable notes. Chris wrote *Home for The Holidays & Other Calamities* (the book from Simon & Schuster). Its title story was made into the perennial holiday favorite, *Home for the Holidays* (directed by Jodie Foster). To read other short pieces by Chris Radant, visit www.bloggietheclown.blogspot.com.

A two-time recipient of the Lambda Book Award for Humor, **David Rakoff** is a regular contributor to Public Radio International's "This American Life" and the *New York Times Magazine*, a correspondent for *Outside*, and Writer-at-Large for *GQ*. His writing has also appeared in *Vogue*, *Salon*, *Seed*, *Condé Nast Traveler*, the *New York Observer*, and *Wired*, among others. He recently contributed the essay on Utah for the 2008 book *State by State: A Panoramic Portrait of America* and is working on a new book entitled *Half Empty*.

David Sedaris is the author of the books *Barrel Fever, Naked, Holidays on Ice, Me Talk Pretty One Day, Dress Your Family in Corduroy and Denim*, and *When You Are Engulfed in Flames*. He is a frequent contributor to the *New Yorker* and can often be heard on Public Radio International's "This American Life."

Charles Simic is a poet, essayist, and translator. He was born in Yugoslavia in 1938 and immigrated to the United States in 1954. Since 1967, he has published twenty books of his own poetry, seven books of essays, a memoir, and numerous translations of French, Serbian, Croatian, Macedonian, and Slovenian poetry. He has received many literary awards, including the Pulitzer Prize, the Griffin Prize, the MacArthur Fellowship, and the Wallace Stevens Award. *Voice at 3:00 A.M.*, a volume of his selected later and new poems, was published by Harcourt in 2003 and a new book of poems, *That Little Something*, was published in the spring of 2008. A former poetry editor of the *Paris Review*, Simic is a frequent contributor to the *New York Review of Books*. He is Emeritus Professor of the University of New Hampshire where he has taught since 1973. He was the fifteenth Poet Laureate of the United States (2007–2008).

Hunter S. Thompson was born and raised in Louisville, Kentucky. His books include *Fear and Loathing in America, Screwjack, Hell's Angels, Fear and Loathing on the Campaign Trail '72, The Curse of Lono, Fear and Loathing in Las Vegas, The Proud Highway, Better Than Sex, Songs of the Doomed*, and *The Rum Diary*. Thompson died in 2005.

James Thurber, one of the outstanding American humorists of the twentieth century, is known for his distinctively funny cartoons and short stories. Though hampered by failing eyesight, Thurber wrote nearly forty books, including collections of essays, short stories, fables, and children's stories. He won a Tony Award for his popular Broadway play, *A Thurber Carnival*, in which he often starred as himself.

Calvin Trillin, who became the *Nation's* "deadline poet" in 1990, has been a staff writer at the *New Yorker* since 1963. He is the author of *Deciding the Next Decider*, *A Heckuva Job*, *Obliviously on He Sails*, and *About Alice*. He has also written verse on the events of the day for the *New Yorker*, the *New York Times*, and National Public Radio. He says he believes in an inclusive political system that prohibits from public office only those whose names have awkward meter or are difficult to rhyme. He lives in New York.

John Waters grew up in Baltimore, where he still lives, and has been making movies since he was seventeen. His films include *Mondo Trasho*, *Multiple Maniacs*, *Pink Flamingos*, *Female Trouble*, *Desperate Living*, *Polyesther*, *Hairspray*, *Cry Baby*, *Serial Mom*, *Pecker*, and *Cecil B. Demented*. The musical adaptation of his film *Hairspray* won eight Tony Awards on Broadway.

CREDITS

"'Tis the Season for Halitosis," from *I Love You More Than You Know* by Jonathan Ames. Copyright © 2006 by Jonathan Ames. Used by permission of Grove/Atlantic, Inc.

"Christmas Shopping: A Survivor's Guide," © 1982 by Dave Barry is reprinted with the author's permission and should not be duplicated.

"Xmas Words," copyright 2008 by Roy Blount, Jr. First published in the *New York Times*. Reprinted here by permission of the author.

The extract from *I Hate Christmas* is published with the kind permission of Allison and Busby, Ltd. Copyright © 2005 by Daniel Blythe.

Selection from *Women* by Charles Bukowski. Copyright © 1978 by Charles Bukowski. Reprinted by permission of HarperCollins Publishers.

"Oh, Christmas Tree," from *Running with Scissors*, by Augusten Burroughs, © 2002 by the author and reprinted by permission of St. Martin's Press, LLC.

"Christmas Is A Sad Season For The Poor," from *The Stories of John Cheever* by John Cheever, copyright © 1978 by John Cheever. Used by permission of Alfred A. Knopf, a division of Random House, Inc. Also published in the U.K. by Jonathan Cape. Reprinted by permission of The Random House Group Ltd.

"Thanksgiving Poems" reprinted by permission of Billy Collins. © 2009 Billy Collins.

Selections from *The Office Party* are reprinted by permission of Harold Ober Associates Incorporated. First published in Esquire. Copyright 1951 by Corey Ford.

"The Terrible Fourth Day of Christmas," by Scott Horton, copyright © 2007 by *Harper's Magazine*. All rights reserved. Reproduced from the December issue by special permission.

Scene 2 from *The Truth About Santa (an apocalyptic holiday tale)*, © 2008 by Greg Kotis. Reprinted by permission of Paradigm Talent and Literary Agency. The stage performance rights for *The Truth About Santa* are controlled by Dramatists Play Service, Inc., www.dramatists.com.

"Christmas Carol," by Lewis Lapham, copyright © 1995 by *Harper's Magazine*. All rights reserved. Reproduced from the December issue by special permission.

Excerpts from *Last Last Chance* by Fiona Maazel. Copyright © 2008 by Fiona Maazel. Reprinted by permission of Farrar, Straus and Giroux, LLC.

"The Madonna of Turkey Season" was reprinted by permission of International Creative Management, Inc. Copyright © 2009 by Jay McInerney.